Knits *from* Northern Lands

Knits *from* Northern Lands

20 Projects Inspired by Traditional Knitting Techniques
from the Scottish Isles to Scandinavia

Jenny Fennell

Interweave

A Quarto Book

Interweave
An imprint of Penguin Random House LLC
penguinrandomhouse.com

Conceived, edited, and designed by
Quarto Publishing plc,
an imprint of the Quarto Group
The Old Brewery
6 Blundell Street
London N7 9BH

QUAR.340563
Printed in Singapore
1 3 5 7 9 10 8 6 4 2

ISBN 9780593331972

Editor: Ruth Patrick
Designer: Rachel Cross
Photographer: Nicole Lapierre
Illustrator: Olya Kamieshkova, Kuo Kang Chen
Pattern checker: Therese Chynoweth
Proofreader: Caroline West
Editorial assistant: Ella Whiting
Art director: Gemma Wilson
Publisher: Samantha Warrington

Contents

Meet Jenny

My name is Jenny Fennell and I live in the countryside of Middle Musquodoboit, Nova Scotia, with my partner Ryan and our two children, Jimmy and Lily.

Most days are spent taking walks through the surrounding Acadian forest on our property, which is home to black bears, bobcats, coyotes, and white-tail deer, or cuddled up with some fiber finishing a project from my never-ending "to knit" pile.

I have grown up seeing my mother and grandmother knit countless pieces but hadn't picked up any needles myself until 2013.

I had traveled to Scotland to visit family, and seeing inside woollen mills during my visit sparked something in me. My love and fascination for knitting and natural fiber really blossomed. I had no idea something so intricate and beautiful could be created with what was shorn from a sheep's back.

Fast-forward, having dipped my toes in everything from fashion design and textile studies to sewing and dressmaking, and I can easily say it is an obsession of mine to craft knitted garments of any and all types. I am drawn to the romantic tales that detailed cable and colourwork can tell, having been inspired by folklore tales of Scottish history. I am determined to create pieces that will be cherished, and when the time comes, a piece that can withstand generations and be passed on to loved ones to be cherished once more.

What I want people to take away from this book is that no one is a natural knitter; everyone learns with practice and patience. I was once an awful knitter who couldn't get past a simple coaster. You just need to stick with it. Whatever project you want to complete, no matter how difficult, just start and go easy on yourself; you're learning something new. Don't unravel, and just keep going. The wonderful thing about the knitting community is that there is always someone willing to help if you are stuck.

When you craft something that takes so much effort, you are more likely to be a little more gentle with it, and mend it if need be. You won't be so quick to replace it and in turn consume more. Once you start treating your clothing in this manner, it overflows into other areas of your life, creating a slower, gentler pace. Wearing a piece you have put so much into means a little more than mass-produced clothing items, and you can feel it when you wear it.

This book is a reminder to slow down, be gentle, and appreciate what you have. Working with your hands is good for your soul.

Tools and Materials

In order to knit your first piece, all you need is a pair of knitting needles, yarn, a tape measure, and a pair of scissors. On the following pages you will find out which tools and materials are used in this book and gain inspiration.

KNITTING NEEDLE TYPES

Various types of knitting needles are available, and the project you are creating determines the type of needles you should use.

Single-pointed needles Widely available and commonly used, single-pointed needles are sold in pairs and have a point at one end and a knurl, knob, or other stopper at the other end to prevent the stitches sliding off. You can use these needles for knitting flat fabrics.

Double-pointed needles These needles have points at both ends and are sold in sets of four or five needles. Often referred to as "dpn," they are used for knitting tubular fabrics such as socks, sweater sleeves, and seamless sweaters (also called knitting in the round).

Circular needles A circular needle comprises two short, single-pointed needles, joined to each other by a flexible cord. The cord may be permanently attached, but there are also sets available with interchangeable needles (tips) and cords of different lengths. My preferred needles would be a set of interchangeable circular needles.

Cable needles Cable needles are short, double-pointed needles that are straight, hook-shaped, or with a kink in the middle. They are used when creating cables as a means of temporarily holding a small number of stitches. Choose a size that is the same as, or slightly smaller than, your main knitting to avoid stretching your cable stitches.

KNITTING NEEDLE MATERIALS

Knitting needles are available in a wide variety of materials, and you will be sure to find a pair that works for you within your budget. You can often pick up needles from thrift stores or upcycling websites such as Freecycle or Craig's List.

Bamboo Bamboo needles are flexible, lightweight, and warm to the touch, making them popular with knitters who have arthritis or rheumatism. Budget bamboo needles can split with use, so buy the best pair within your budget. They can be lightly sanded with sandpaper if rough spots appear.

Wood There are many beautiful wooden needles on the market and many knitters find these the most comfortable to work with because they are warm, light, and easy on the hands. Like bamboo they may break, but can be sanded with care.

Metal Many knitters prefer metal needles because they are virtually indestructible. They are the needles of choice for many lace knitters because they have the sharpest points for fine work. The smooth finish also makes them a popular choice for knitting at speed. Prices vary significantly for metal needles.

YARNS

Here is a summary of the types of yarn used to create the projects in this book. The specific yarns can be found in the materials lists for each project.

No. 1 Super Fine (fingering) weight Shetland Sheep Wool Known for being durable and hardy, this 2-ply fiber is perfect if you are looking to create a lacework, Fair Isle, or sweater project.

No. 3 Light weight Sport Peruvian Highland Sheep Wool Ideally used for colorwork projects and fine gauge pieces.

No. 3 Light/No. 4. Medium weight Superwash Wool A natural superwash fiber is a popular choice as it is easy to care for, being machine washable and dryable, unlike most natural wools.

No. 4 Medium weight Peruvian Highland Sheep Wool The versatility of this fiber makes it a great choice for a wide range of projects that will give great stitch definition.

No. 5 Bulky weight Peruvian Highland Sheep Wool Natural wool is always a great idea. You don't have to worry about any harsh chemicals in the fiber, but can rest assured that it is compostable and won't damage the Earth.

No. 5 Bulky weight Icelandic Sheep Wool The Icelandic sheep breed has been isolated on the island for more than 1,100 years. During this time they have adapted to the harsh Arctic climate, which makes their wool distinct from any other. Use this fiber for pieces to keep you warm in very cold temperatures.

No. 5 Bulky weight Bolivian Merino Wool This super-soft fiber is perfect for projects that need an extra bit of softness. Use for pieces that will be next to your skin, such as hats, scarves, or sweaters.

No. 6 Super Bulky/No. 7 Jumbo weight Peruvian Highland Sheep Wool Your projects will take no time to craft as each stitch is roughly ½in (1cm).

USEFUL TOOLS FOR KNITTERS

In addition to your knitting needles, there are a few items that you will find very useful, and a small number that are essential.

Pen and notepad These essential knitting bag items are useful for marking off where you are in a pattern and making notes about patterns and any alterations you may have made. If you reach the stage where you are designing your own knits, jot down any thoughts, ideas, and inspiration for these and future projects.

Scissors Choose small scissors with sharp points because these will allow you to cut neatly and in the right place. It is worth investing in good-quality scissors, since inexpensive ones may snag your knitted fabric. Keep them in a pouch or case to prevent accidents.

Tapestry needle Needles with sharper points, such as the type used for needlepoint or tapestry, are useful for sewing in ends where you need to split the yarn. Sewing needles can also be used for adding buttons, zippers, and other accessories. Select a size to suit the thickness of your yarn.

Tape measure Use a tape measure for body measurements and for measuring any knitted piece's progress.

Scrap yarn This is useful for holding stitches, marking key stages in your knitting, indicating the location of pattern repeats, and for specific techniques, such as provisional cast on and lifelines.

Pins Pins are used to hold your knitting together when assembling. Choose large-headed pins where possible so that you can see them easily. A selection of longer pins for longer seams and shorter pins for smaller areas will be useful.

Stitch markers Ranging from inexpensive plastic to beautiful, handmade beaded sets, stitch markers denote key points in your knitting; for example, marking the end of a round or pattern repeat. Choose a size slightly larger than your needles, checking that they slide easily and that any beads won't catch in your work.

Clip-in markers These are similar to stitch markers but with an open end, allowing them to be inserted and removed anywhere at any time. Useful for marking key points in your work when you need to leave the marker in the work and return to it later.

The Projects

*In this chapter you will find everything you need to help you create
the twenty beautiful projects featured in the book, remembering
traditions of the past and starting heirlooms of your own, all
inspired by the lands of the North.*

Wrapped in Rib Scarf

Knitted garments have always been a traditional way of staying warm in the Celtic, Scandinavian, and Icelandic regions. Over time, knitters of the northern lands perfected certain stitches to provide more warmth. The rib stitch acts as a double layer of protection against the cold. With a beginner knitter in mind, this ribbed scarf pattern is a perfect starting point in your Northern knitting journey.

SKILL LEVEL ✕

GAUGE
- 16 sts and 13 rows = 4in (10cm) in k2, p2 rib

NEEDLES
- U.S. size 15 (10mm)

Adjust needle size if necessary to obtain the correct gauge.

YARN
- Super Bulky weight (#6 Super Bulky)

Shown in: Cascade Yarns Magnum (100% Peruvian Highland wool; 123yd [112.5m]/8.82oz [250g]); #8012 Doeskin Heather, 3 skeins

NOTIONS
- Tapestry needle

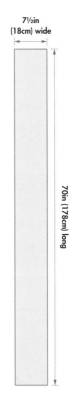

7½in (18cm) wide

70in (178cm) long

SCARF

CO 30 sts.

ROW 1 (RS): *p2, k2; rep from * 6 more times, p2.
ROW 2 (WS): *k2, p2; rep from * 6 more times, k2.

Rep Rows 1 and 2 until piece measures 70in (178cm).

BO loosely in patt.

FINISHING
Weave in ends. Block lightly if desired.

ABBREVIATIONS FOR SCARF

BO bind off.
CO cast on.
K knit.
P purl.
Patt pattern.

Rep repeat.
RS right side of work.
St/s stitch/es.
WS wrong side of work.

Wrapped in Rib Hat

The rib stitch has traditionally been used to make items such as scarves, hats, and sweaters. This type of hat would be a staple piece in a fisherman's wardrobe. Using the rib stitch, in the same way that knitters of the past would to give their loved ones who were heading out to sea, this seamless hat pattern is a simple and quick knit that you will certainly appreciate on a cold day.

SKILL LEVEL 人

GAUGE
- 11 sts and 11 rnds = 4in (10cm) in k1, p1 rib

NEEDLES
- U.S. size 15 (10mm), 16in (40cm) circular, and set of 4 or 5 double-pointed

Adjust needle size if necessary to obtain the correct gauge.

YARN
- Super Bulky weight (#6 Super Bulky)

Shown in: Cascade Yarns Magnum (100% Peruvian Highland wool; 123yd [112.5m]/8.82oz [250g]); #8012 Doeskin Heather, 1 skein

NOTIONS
- Stitch marker
- Tapestry needle

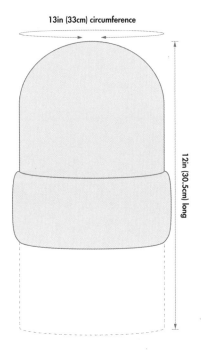

13in (33cm) circumference

12in (30.5cm) long

HAT

With cir needle, CO 36 sts.

Pm and join for working in rnds, being careful not to twist sts.

RND 1: *k1, p1; rep from * to end of rnd.

Rep Rnd 1 until piece measures approx. 11¼in (28.5cm), or ¾in (2cm) short of desired length.

SHAPE TOP
Change to dpn.

DEC'D RND 1: k1, *k2tog; rep from * to last st, k1—19 sts rem.
DEC'D RND 2: *k2tog, k1; rep from * to last st, k1—13 sts rem.

Cut yarn, leaving a 10in (25cm) long tail, thread tail through rem sts, pulling tightly to close hole, and fasten off on WS.

FINISHING
Weave in ends. Lightly block if desired.

ABBREVIATIONS FOR HAT

Cir circular.
CO cast on.
Dec'd decreased
Dpn/s double-pointed needle/s.
K knit.
K2tog knit 2 sts together.

P purl.
Pm place marker.
Rem remaining.
RS right side of work.
Rnd/s round/s.
St/s stitch/es.
WS wrong side of work.

Wrapped in Rib Fingerless Mitts

These beautiful cozy mitts are knitted in rib stitch to complete the set, along with the Rib Scarf (see page 17) and Rib Hat (see page 19). Continue the knitting tradition of creating a piece with a loved one in mind, or treat yourself to toasty hands on a cold winter's day. You will add seaming to your list of techniques, which will also come in useful later in the book.

SKILL LEVEL ⟋

GAUGE
- 11 sts and 12 rows = 4in (10cm) in k1, p1 rib

NEEDLES
- U.S. size 15 (10mm)

Adjust needle size if necessary to obtain the correct gauge.

YARN
- Super bulky weight (#6 Super Bulky)

Shown in: Cascade Yarns Magnum (100% Peruvian Highland wool; 123yd [112.5m]/8.82oz [250g]); #8012 Doeskin Heather, 1 skein

NOTIONS
- Tapestry needle

5½in (14cm) circumference

7½in (19cm) long

MITTS

CO 17 sts, leaving a 14in (35.5cm) long tail for seaming.

ROW 1 (RS): *k1, p1; rep from * 7 more times, k1.
ROW 2 (WS): *p1, k1; rep from * 7 more times, p1.

Rep Rows 1 and 2 until piece measures 7½in (19cm).

BO loosely in patt, leaving an 8in (20.5cm) long tail for seaming.

FINISHING
With RS facing, fold side edges of mitt toward the center (WS now facing, and RS is to inside).

Using long CO tail, sew edges tog from bottom up for approx. 3½in (9cm) using mattress st (see opposite). Fasten off.

Using long BO tail, sew edges tog from top down for approx. 2in (5cm) using mattress st, leaving approx. 2in (5cm) open for thumb opening.

Fasten off.

Weave in ends. Lightly block if desired.

ABBREVIATIONS FOR MITTS

BO bind off.	**Rep** repeat.
CO cast on.	**RS** right side of work.
K knit.	**St/s** stitch/es.
P purl.	**Tog** together.
Patt pattern.	**WS** wrong side of work.

MATTRESS STITCH SEAMING

1. Lay the two pieces you want to seam with the wrong side facing down. Thread a darning needle and insert into the first knit stitch on the right-side piece, threading the yarn through.

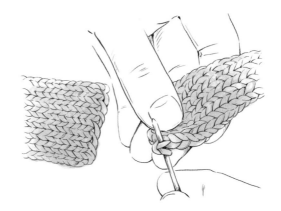

2. Insert the darning needle into the first stitch on the left-side piece, threading the yarn through.

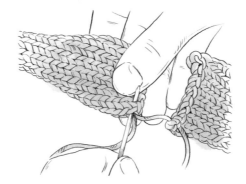

3. Continue to thread the yarn through the right and left pieces, pulling the yarn tight every couple of stitches to tighten up the seam.

4. Repeat steps 1 to 3 until you have seamed together all the stitches. Tie a knot at the end to secure and weave in the ends.

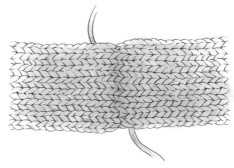

Dream in Danish Throw Pillow

When knitting first took hold in Scandinavia, families in Denmark would generally have a sweater piece for each member. Back then, throwaway culture was unheard of; the zero-waste lifestyle was everyday life. Once a family member had outgrown a sweater, it would be passed down. When it became too worn out to wear, it was fashioned into pillow covers or blankets. This simple knit and purl piece is so easy that you'll want to craft one for each of your own family members.

SKILL LEVEL X

GAUGE
- 22½ sts and 32 rnds = 4in (10cm) in stockinette st

NEEDLES
- U.S. size 3 (3.25mm), 24in (60cm) circular

Adjust needle size if necessary to obtain the correct gauge.

YARN
- Worsted weight (#4 Medium)

Shown in: Cascade 220 Heathers (100% Peruvian Highland wool; 220yd [200m]/3½oz [100g]); #2452 Turtle, 2 skeins

NOTIONS
- Stitch marker, tapestry needle, 16in (40cm) pillow, 14in (35.5cm) long zipper (optional)

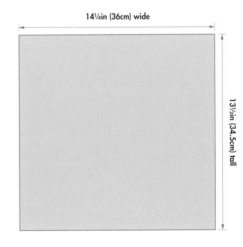

14¼in (36cm) wide

13½in (34.5cm) tall

PILLOW

CO 160 sts. Pm and join for working
in rnds, being careful not to twist sts.

Work Rnds 1–42 of Chart A, or as foll:
RNDS 1–3: *k1, p1; rep from * to end of rnd.
RND 4: Purl.
RND 5: Knit.
RND 6: Purl.
RND 7: *p1, k7; rep from * to end of rnd.
RND 8: *k1, p1, k5, p1; rep from * to end of rnd.
RND 9: *k2, p1, k3, p1, k1; rep from * to end of rnd.
RND 10: *k3, p1, k1, p1, k2; rep from * to end of rnd.
RND 11: *k4, p1, k3; rep from * to end of rnd.
RND 12: Rep Rnd 10.
RND 13: Rep Rnd 9.
RND 14: Rep Rnd 8.
RND 15: Rep Rnd 7.
RND 16: Purl.
RND 17: Knit.
RND 18: Purl.
RNDS 19–21: Knit.
RND 22: *k1, p1; rep from * to end of rnd.
RNDS 23–25: Knit.
RND 26: *p1, k1; rep from * to end of rnd.
RNDS 27–29: Knit.
RND 30: Purl.
RND 31: Knit.
RND 32: Purl.
RNDS 33 and 34: *k1, p1; rep from * to end of rnd.
RNDS 35–38: Rep Rnds 31–34.
RNDS 39 and 41: Knit.
RNDS 40 and 42: Purl.

Work Rnds 1–29 of Chart B, or as foll:
RND 1: *k6, p1, k27, p1, k5; rep from * to end of rnd.

RND 2: *k7, p1, k25, p1, k6; rep from * to end of rnd.
RND 3: *k8, p1, k23, p1, k7; rep from * to end of rnd.
RND 4: *k9, p1, k21, p1, k8; rep from * to end of rnd.
RND 5: *k10, p1, k19, p1, k9; rep from * to end of rnd.
RND 6: *k3, p1, k7, p1, k17, p1, k7, p1, k2; rep from * to end of rnd.
RND 7: *k2, p2, k8, p1, k15, p1, k8, p2, k1; rep from * to end of rnd.
RND 8: *k1, p3, k9, p1, k13, p1, k9, p3; rep from * to end of rnd.
RND 9: *p4, k10, p1, k11, p1, k10, p3; rep from * to end of rnd.
RND 10: *p4, k11, p1, k9, p1, k11, p3; rep from * to end of rnd.
RND 11: *p3, k13, p1, k7, p1, k13, p2; rep from * to end of rnd.
RND 12: *p2, k3, p5, k7, p1, k5, p1, k7, p5, k3, p1; rep from * to end of rnd.
RND 13: *p1, k3, p5, k9, p1, k3, p1, k9, p5, k3; rep from * to end of rnd.
RND 14: *k3, p5, k11, p1, k1, p1, k11, p5, k2; rep from * to end of rnd.
RND 15: *k2, p5, k13, p1, k13, p5, k1; rep from * to end of rnd.
RND 16: *k3, p5, k11, p1, k1, p1, k11, p5, k2; rep from * to end of rnd.
RND 17: *p1, k3, p5, k9, p1, k3, p1, k9, p5, k3; rep from * to end of rnd.
RND 18: *p2, k3, p5, k7, p1, k5, p1, k7, p5, k3, p1; rep from * to end of rnd.
RND 19: *p3, k13, p1, k7, p1, k13, p2; rep from * to end of rnd.
RND 20: *p4, k11, p1, k9, p1, k11, p3; rep from * to end of rnd.
RND 21: *p4, k10, p1, k11, p1, k10, p3; rep from * to end of rnd.

ABBREVIATIONS FOR PILLOW

BO bind off.
CO cast on.
Foll follows.
K knit.
Kwise knitwise.

P purl.
Pm place marker.
Rep repeat.
Rnd/s round/s.
St/s stitch/es.

Tog together.

RND 22: *k1, p3, k9, p1, k13, p1, k9, p3; rep from * to end of rnd.

RND 23: *k2, p2, k8, p1, k15, p1, k8, p2, k1; rep from * to end of rnd.

RND 24: *k3, p1, k7, p1, k17, p1, k7, p1, k2; rep from * to end of rnd.

RND 25: *k10, p1, k19, p1, k9; rep from * to end of rnd.

RND 26: *k9, p1, k21, p1, k8; rep from * to end of rnd.

RND 27: *k8, p1, k23, p1, k7; rep from * to end of rnd.

RND 28: *k7, p1, k25, p1, k6; rep from * to end of rnd.

RND 29: *k6, p1, k27, p1, k5; rep from * to end of rnd.

Work Rnds 1–42 of Chart C, or as foll:

RND 1: Purl.

RND 2: Knit.

RND 3: Purl.

RNDS 4 and 5: *k1, p1; rep from * to end of rnd.

RNDS 6–9: Rep Rnds 2–5.

RNDS 10 and 12: Knit.

RNDS 11 and 13: Purl.

NOTES

The pillow cover is worked to smaller dimensions than the pillow form to get a snug fit over the form when finished.

When switching from knit stitches to purl stitches your gauge can sometimes become a little loose, causing a gap or a wonky stitch. To help close the gap and straighten out your knits and purls, when you are switching from a knit stitch to a purl stitch, instead of bringing your yarn in front to purl the next stitch, keep your yarn in back (as if you were going to work another knit stitch), give it a little tug to tighten things up, then bring your yarn to the front and work your purl as you normally would. This little trick will make all the difference in cleaning up your gauge when going back and forth from knits to purls!

See overleaf for pattern

RNDS 14–16: Knit.

RND 17: *k1, p1; rep from * to end of rnd.

RNDS 18–20: Knit.

RND 21: *p1, k1; rep from * to end of rnd.

RNDS 22–24: Knit.

RND 25: Purl.

RND 26: Knit.

RND 27: Purl.

RND 28: *p1, k7; rep from * to end of rnd.

RND 29: *k1, p1, k5, p1; rep from * to end of rnd.

RND 30: *k2, p1, k3, p1, k1; rep from * to end of rnd.

RND 31: *k3, p1, k1, p1, k2; rep from * to end of rnd.

RND 32: *k4, p1, k3; rep from * to end of rnd.

RND 33: Rep Rnd 31.

RND 34: Rep Rnd 30.

RND 35: Rep Rnd 29.

RND 36: Rep Rnd 28.

RND 37: Purl.

CHART KEY

- ☐ knit
- ▪ purl
- ☐ pattern repeat

CHART A

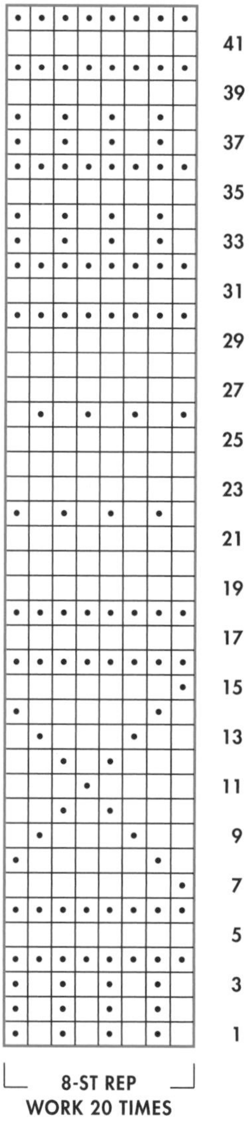

8-ST REP
WORK 20 TIMES

CHART C

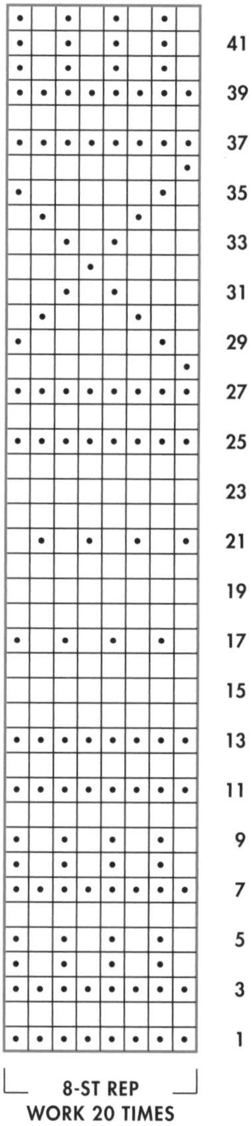

8-ST REP
WORK 20 TIMES

RND 38: Knit.

RND 39: Purl.

RNDS 40–42: *k1, p1; rep from * to end of rnd.

BO kwise.

FINISHING

Weave in ends. Block to 15½in (39.5cm) wide and 15½in (39.5cm) tall; the piece will relax to the finished measurements after blocking.

Sew one end closed using mattress st (see page 25).

Insert pillow and sew remaining end closed using mattress st, or center zipper in opening and sew in place, making sure to sew ends of opening tog using mattress st.

CHART B

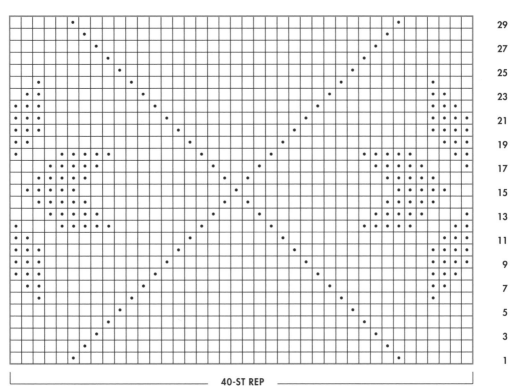

40-ST REP
WORK 4 TIMES

Lace of Unst Bookmark

The Shetland Islands are a cluster of about 100 islands between Scotland and Norway, some with knitting traditions specific to each island. Fair Isle to the South is known for its intricate colorwork knitting, while the northern isle of Unst is known for fine lacework. This quick-knit bookmark acts as a perfect practice run for lace knitting.

SKILL LEVEL ✕✕

GAUGE
- 25 sts and 32 rows = 4in (10cm) in stockinette st

NEEDLES
- U.S. size 3 (3.25mm)

Adjust needle size if necessary to obtain the correct gauge.

YARN
- Fingering weight (#1 Super Fine)

Shown in: Jamieson & Smith 2-ply Jumper Weight (100% Shetland wool; 125yd [115m]/.88oz [25g]); #202 Stone, 1 ball

NOTIONS
- Tapestry needle

2in (5cm) wide

7¼in (18.5cm) long

BOOKMARK

CO 13 sts.

Work Rows 1–8 of Chart, or as foll:
ROW 1 (RS): k2, yo, k3, sk2p, k3, yo, k2.
ROWS 2, 4, and 6 (WS): Purl.
ROW 3: k3, yo, k2, sk2p, k2, yo, k3.
ROW 5: k4, yo, k1, sk2p, k1, yo, k4.
ROW 7: k5, yo, sk2p, yo, k5.
ROW 8: Purl.

Rep Rows 1–8 five more times.

SHAPE TOP
Work Rows 9–16 of Chart, or as foll:
ROW 9 (DEC'D): k1, skp, k7, k2tog, k1—11 sts rem.
ROW 10 (DEC'D): p1, p2tog, p5, p2tog tbl, p1—9 sts rem.
ROW 11 (DEC'D): k1, skp, k3, k2tog, k1—7 sts rem.
ROW 12 (DEC'D): p1, p2tog, p1, p2tog tbl, p1—5 sts rem.
ROW 13 (DEC'D): k1, skp, k2—4 sts rem.
ROW 14 (DEC'D): p1, p2tog, p1—3 sts rem.
ROW 15 (DEC'D): k1, skp—2 sts rem.
ROW 16 (DEC'D): p2tog—1 st rem.

Fasten off rem st.

FINISHING
Weave in ends. Block to measurements.

CHART KEY

☐	k on RS, p on WS
⊙	yo
╱	k2tog on RS, p2tog on WS
╲	skp on RS, p2tog tbl on WS
⋏	sk2p
☐	pattern repeat

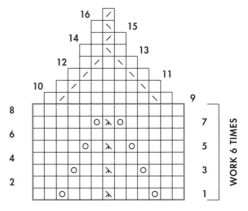

ABBREVIATIONS FOR BOOKMARK

CO cast on.
Dec'd decreased.
Foll follows.
K knit.
K2tog knit 2 sts together.
P purl.

P2tog purl 2 sts together.
P2tog tbl purl 2 sts together through the back loop.
Rem remaining.
Rep repeat.
RS right side of work.

Sk2p slip 1 st knitwise, k2tog, pass slipped st over.
Skp slip, knit, pass. Slip next st knitwise, knit the next st, pass the slipped st over the knit st.
St/s stitch/es.

WS wrong side of work.
Yo hold yarn in front of work.

Mira Mhór Cowl

Knots, spirals, plaits, and braids were used in Celtic culture as early as the fourth century. Knots are made up of loops that have no start or finish, representing eternity. Love knots, on which the cable in this pattern is based, were exchanged by couples just as rings are today. This pattern is great if you are new to cable work and will work up quickly, giving you the practice and confidence to tackle larger cable work pieces.

SKILL LEVEL XX

GAUGE
- 16 sts and 15 rows = 4in (10cm) in pattern

NEEDLES
- U.S. size 11 (8mm)

Adjust needle size if necessary to obtain the correct gauge

YARN
- Super Bulky weight (#6 Super Bulky)

Shown in: Cascade Yarns Magnum (100% Peruvian Highland wool; 123yd [112.5m]/8.82oz [250g]); #9564 Birch Heather, 1 hank

NOTIONS
- Cable needle
- Tapestry needle

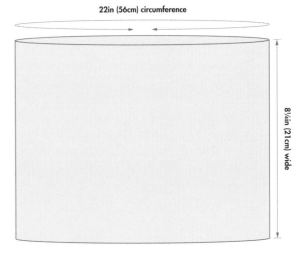

22in (56cm) circumference

8¼in (21cm) wide

COWL

CO 34 sts.

Work Rows 1–16 of Chart, or as foll:

ROW 1 (RS): k3, p4, (2/2 RC, p4) 3 times, k3.

ROW 2 (WS): p3, (k4, p4) 3 times, k4, p3.

ROW 3: k3, p3, 2/1 RPC, (2/2 LPC, 2/2 RPC) twice, 2/1 LPC, p3, k3.

ROW 4: p3, k3, p2, k3, p4, k4, p4, k3, p2, k3, p3.

ROW 5: k3, p2, 2/1 RPC, p3, 2/2 LC, p4, 2/2 LC, p3, 2/1 LPC, p2, k3.

ROW 6: p3, k2, p2, (k4, p4) twice, k4, p2, k2, p3.

ROW 7: k3, p2, k2, p3, 2/1 RPC, 2/2 LPC, 2/2 RPC, 2/1 LPC, p3, k2, p2, k3.

ROW 8: p3, k2, (p2, k3) twice, p4, (k3, p2) twice, k2, p3.

ROW 9: k3, p2, (k2, p3) twice, 2/2 RC, (p3, k2) twice, p2, k3.

ROW 10: Rep Row 8.

ROW 11: k3, p2, k2, p3, 2/1 LPC, 2/2 RPC, 2/2 LPC, 2/1 RPC, p3, k2, p2, k3.

ROW 12: Rep Row 6.

ROW 13: k3, p2, 2/1 LPC, p3, 2/2 LC, p4, 2/2 LC, p3, 2/1 RPC, p2, k3.

ROW 14: Rep Row 4.

ROW 15: k3, p3, 2/1 LPC, (2/2 RPC, 2/2 LPC) twice, 2/1 RPC, p3, k3.

ROW 16: p3, (k4, p4) 3 times, k4, p3.

Rep Rows 1–16 three more times, then work Rows 1–15 once more, making sure at least 3yd (2.8m) of yarn rem. Piece should measure approx. 22in (56cm) from beg.

BO all sts in patt.

STITCH GUIDE

2/1 LPC (2 OVER 1 LEFT PURL CROSS): Sl 2 sts to cn and hold in front, p1, then k2 from cn *(see page 120)*.

2/1 RPC (2 OVER 1 RIGHT PURL CROSS): Sl 1 st to cn and hold in back, k2, then p1 from cn *(see page 119)*.

2/2 LC (2 OVER 2 LEFT CROSS): Sl 2 sts to cn and hold in front, k2, then k2 from cn *(see page 122)*.

2/2 LPC (2 OVER 2 LEFT PURL CROSS): Sl 2 sts to cn and hold in front, p2, then k2 from cn *(see page 124)*.

2/2 RC (2 OVER 2 RIGHT CROSS): Sl 2 sts to cn and hold in back, k2, then k2 from cn *(see page 121)*.

2/2 RPC (2 OVER 2 RIGHT PURL CROSS): Sl 2 sts to cn and hold in back, k2, then p2 from cn *(see page 123)*.

FINISHING

Weave in ends. Block to measurements.

Join ends using mattress st *(see page 25)*.

ABBREVIATIONS FOR COWL

Beg beginning.	**K** knit.	**RS** right side of work.
BO bind off.	**P** purl.	**Sl** slip.
Cn cable needle.	**Patt** pattern.	**St/s** stitch/es.
CO cast on.	**Rem** remaining.	**WS** wrong side of work.
Foll follows.	**Rep** repeat.	

CHART KEY

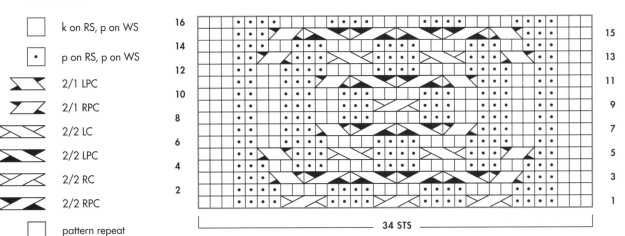

□	k on RS, p on WS
⊡	p on RS, p on WS
⟋	2/1 LPC
⟍	2/1 RPC
⟋	2/2 LC
⟋	2/2 LPC
⟍	2/2 RC
⟍	2/2 RPC
□	pattern repeat

34 STS

Leaves of Birch Blanket

Inspired by Old Scottish lore that tells tales of mothers hanging birch leaves over their children's beds at night to prevent nightmares and visits from mischievous fairies while they slept, this beautiful blanket is slightly easier to craft than some of the featured projects, yet the slipped stitch technique lends a beautiful detail to what will become a treasured piece.

SKILL LEVEL ✕✕

GAUGE
- 21.5 sts and 24 rows = 4in (10cm) in pattern

NEEDLES
- U.S. size 7 (4.5mm), 36in (90cm) circular

Adjust needle size if necessary to obtain the correct gauge.

YARN
- Bulky weight (#5 Bulky)

Shown in: Cascade Eco+ (100% Peruvian Highland wool; 478yd [437m]/8.82oz [250g]); #2452 Turtle, 2 skeins

NOTIONS
- Tapestry needle

26½in (67.5cm) wide

33¼in (84.5cm) long

BLANKET

CO 137 sts. Do not join.

ROWS 1 AND 15 (WS): k2, p1, k2, *p7, k2, p1, k2; rep from * to end.

ROW 2 (RS): p2, yo, k1, yo, p2, *skp, k3, k2tog, p2, yo, k1, yo, p2; rep from * to end—2 sts inc'd.

ROWS 3 and 13: k2, p3, k2, *p5, k2, p3, k2; rep from * to end.

ROW 4: p2, (k1, yo) twice, k1, p2, *skp, k1, k2tog, p2, (k1, yo) twice, k1, p2; rep from * to end—2 sts inc'd.

ROWS 5 and 11: k2, p5, k2, *p3, k2, p5, k2; rep from * to end.

ROW 6: p2, k2, yo, k1, yo, k2, p2, * sk2p, p2, k2, yo, k1, yo, k2, p2; rep from * to end—2 sts inc'd.

ROW 7: k2, p7, k2, *p1, k2, p7, k2; rep from * to end.

ROW 8: p2, *k7, p5; rep from * to last 9 sts, k7, p2.

ROW 9: k2, *p7, k5; rep from * to last 9 sts, p7, k2.

ROW 10: p2, skp, k3, k2tog, p2, *yo, k1, yo, p2, skp, k3, k2tog, p2; rep from * to end—2 sts dec'd.

ROW 12: p2, skp, k1, k2tog, p2, * (k1, yo) twice, k1, p2, skp, k1, k2tog, p2; rep from * to end—2 sts dec'd.

ROW 14: p2, sk2p, p2, * k2, yo, k1, yo, k2, p2, sk2p, p2; rep from * to end—2 sts dec'd.

ROW 16: p5, *k7, p5; rep from * to end.

ROW 17: k5, *p7, k5; rep from * to end.

Rep Rows 2–17 eleven more times, or until piece measures approx. 28in (71cm) from beg.

Work Rows 2–7 once more.

BO in patt.

FINISHING

Weave in ends but do not trim. Block to 30in (76cm) wide and 38in (96.5cm) long; piece will relax to finished measurements after blocking.

Trim ends.

Leaves of Birch Blanket

CHART KEY

☐	k on RS, p on WS
▫•	p on RS, p on WS
○	yo
╱	k2tog
╲	skp
⅄	sk2p
☐	pattern repeat

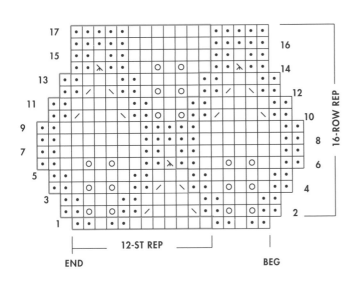

16-ROW REP

12-ST REP

END   BEG

Skies of Sweden Throw Pillow

In the northern regions of Sweden there is a considerable amount of snowfall during the winter months, and with over half of Sweden covered in forest, snow is often seen glistening on the tops of spruce and pine trees. With only two strands of color, this snow-covered scene is an easy place to start your colorwork practice and perhaps have you longing to see the sparkling treetops for yourself.

SKILL LEVEL ✗✗✗

GAUGE
- 21 sts and 25 rnds = 4in (10cm) in colorwork charts

NEEDLES
- U.S. size 7 (4.5mm), 36in (90cm) circular

Adjust needle size if necessary to obtain the correct gauge.

YARN
- Worsted weight (#4 Medium)

Shown in: Cascade 220 Heathers (100% Peruvian wool; 220yds [200m]/3½oz [100g]); #9600 Antiqued Heather (MC), 1 skein; Cascade 220 Superwash Effects (100% superwash wool; 220yds [200m]/3½oz [100g]); #13 Lava (CC), 1 skein

NOTIONS
- Stitch marker
- Tapestry needle
- 18 x 18in (46 x 46cm) pillow insert

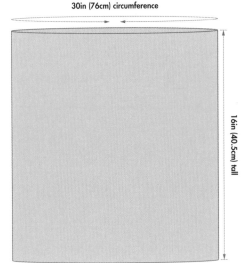

30in (76cm) circumference

16in (40.5cm) tall

PILLOW

With MC, CO 160 sts. Pm and join to work in the rnd, being careful not to twist sts.

Knit 1 rnd.

Join CC. Work Rnds 1–20 of Chart A.

Knit 2 rnds with MC.

Work Rnds 1–30 of Chart B.

Knit 1 rnd with MC.

Work Rnds 1–23 of Chart C.

Knit 2 rnds with MC.

Work Rnds 1–20 of Chart D. Cut CC.

Knit 1 rnd with MC.

BO kwise.

FINISHING

Weave in ends. Block to 16in x 16in (40 x 40cm).

Sew one end closed using mattress st (see page 25).

Insert pillow and sew rem edge closed.

NOTES

This pillow is worked in the round using stranded colorwork. You may find it easier to work the charted patterns by placing a marker at the end of every pattern repeat, using a marker in a unique color for the beginning of the round; Charts A, C, and D all have 20-stitch repeats, while Chart B has a 40-stitch repeat. Slip markers as you come to them.

When working plain rounds within each of the charts and between charts, do not cut the unused color unless instructed to do so. Instead, loosely carry the unused color up along the WS of the work until needed again.

ABBREVIATIONS FOR PILLOW

BO bind off.
CC contrasting color.
CO cast on.
Kwise knitwise.
MC main color.

Pm place marker.
Rem remaining.
Rnd/s round/s.
St/s stitch/es.

CHART KEY

 MC

CC

pattern repeat

CHART A

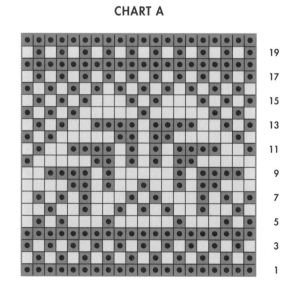

19
17
15
13
11
9
7
5
3
1

CHART B

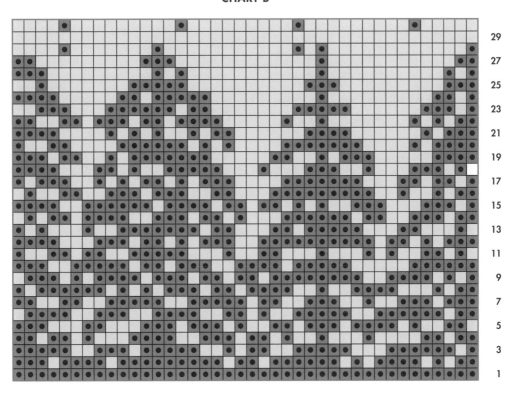

CHART C

CHART D

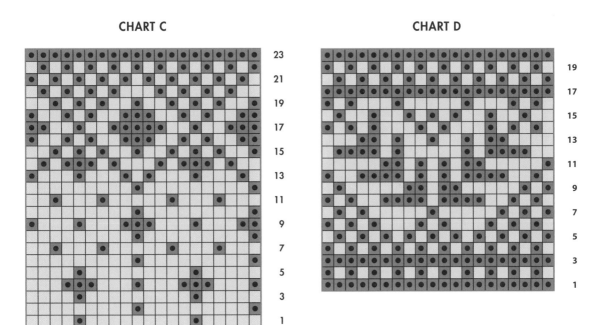

Flowers of Finland Headband

Finland is known for its intricate and bold colorwork knitting. This pattern maintains the Finnish tradition by using a bold blue to showcase Finland's national colours as well as the national flower, lily of the valley. Worked in the round, this two-strand colorwork piece will add extra warmth with a stunning pop of color.

SKILL LEVEL ✕✕✕

GAUGE
- **Version A:** 25 sts and 25 rnds = 4in (10cm) in colorwork charts
- **Version B:** 30 sts and 26 rnds = 4in (10cm) in colorwork charts

NEEDLES
- **Version A:** U.S. size 4 (3.5mm) set of 4 or 5 double-pointed needles or 32in (80cm) long circular needle for Magic Loop method
- **Version B:** U.S. size 3 (3.25mm) set of 4 or 5 double-pointed needles or 32in (80cm) long circular needle for Magic Loop method

Adjust needle size if necessary to obtain the correct gauge.

YARN
- **Version A (cobalt blue and white):** DK weight (#3 Light)/Worsted weight (#4 Medium)

Shown in: Cascade 220 Superwash (100% superwash wool; 220yd [200m]/3½oz [100g]); #875 Feather Gray (MC) and #1025 Cobalt Heather (CC), 1 skein each

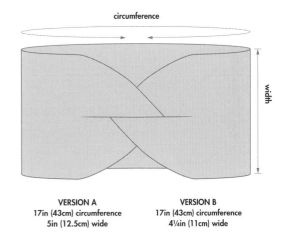

VERSION A
17in (43cm) circumference
5in (12.5cm) wide

VERSION B
17in (43cm) circumference
4¼in (11cm) wide

- **Version B (purple and gray):** Sport weight (#3 Light)

Shown in: Cascade 220 Sport (100% Peruvian Highland wool; 164yd [150m]/1¾oz [50g]); #9691 Violet Tulip (MC) and #8012 Doeskin Heather (CC), 1 skein each

NOTIONS
- Stitch marker
- Tapestry needle

HEADBAND

With appropriate size needles for your version and MC, CO 64 sts. Pm and join to work in the rnd, being careful not to twist sts.

Join CC.

VERSION A
Work Rnds 1–32 of Chart A until piece measures approx. 20in (51cm) from beg, or 1in (2.5cm) less than head circumference.

VERSION B
Work Rnds 1–8 of Chart B until piece measures approx. 20in (51cm) from beg, or 1in (2.5cm) less than head circumference.

BOTH VERSIONS
Cut CC.

BO in MC.

FINISHING
Weave in ends.

VERSION A
Block piece to 20in (51cm) long and 5in (12.5cm) wide.

VERSION B
Block piece to 20in (51cm) long and 4¼in (11cm) wide.

BOTH VERSIONS
Sew ends tog following twist seaming instructions (see page 56).

NOTES

Two versions of this headband are shown; make sure to use the correct yarn weight, needle sizes, and chart for each. Check that you have the correct gauge for the version you are making.

This headband is worked in the round in a long tube, then the ends of the tube are sewn together.

Double-pointed needles, a long circular needle for working the Magic Loop method, or desired needles for small circumference knitting can be used.

There are several rows in Chart A where the unused yarn is floated behind more than four stitches before being used again. Weave in the unused yarn when the float is more than four stitches wide, and be sure not to weave it in over the same stitch every round.

ABBREVIATIONS FOR HEADBAND

Beg beginning.	**CO** cast on.	**Rnd/s** round/s.
BO bind off.	**MC** main color.	**St/s** stitch/es.
CC contrasting color.	**Pm** place marker.	**Tog** together.

TWIST SEAMING

1. With a tapestry needle, seam each open end of the headband closed using mattress stitch (see page 25).

2. Fold the seamed ends in half and hold side by side.

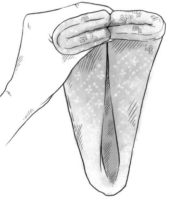

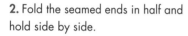

3. Layer half of each folded end into one another.

4. Sew the two ends together in this position, and turn the piece inside out to complete.

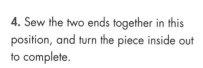

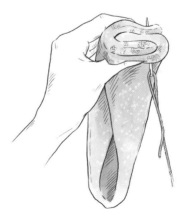

CHART KEY

- ■ MC
- · CC
- □ pattern repeat

CHART B

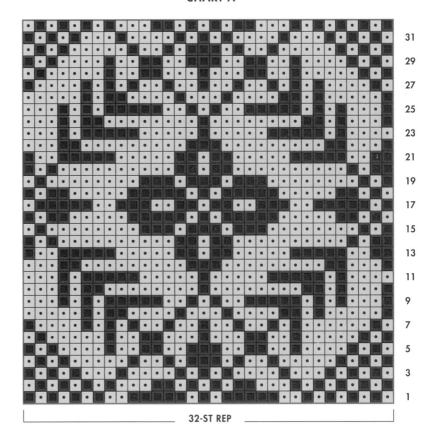

CHART KEY

- · MC
- ■ CC
- □ pattern repeat

CHART A

White Heather Shawl

This gorgeous shawl is inspired by an old Celtic tale of Malvina who was to marry her one true love, until he was slain in battle. As her tears fell upon the heather on the moor she walked though, the purple heather began to turn an enchanting white. As she watched the change she wished this white heather would bring love to whomever came across it. With lacework and bobbles, this shawl is a romantic piece you can drape over your shoulders while thinking about your loved ones.

SKILL LEVEL ✕✕

GAUGE
- 9½ sts and 14 rows = 4in (10cm) in pattern, with yarn held double

NEEDLES
- U.S. size 11 (8mm), 36in (90cm) circular

Adjust needle size if necessary to obtain the correct gauge.

YARN
- Bulky weight (#5 Bulky)

Shown in: Cascade Eco+ Merino (100% Bolivian merino wool; 478 yd [437 m]/8.75oz [250g]); #12 Ecru, 4 skeins

NOTIONS
- Tapestry needle

24½in (62cm) wide

65in (165cm) long

SHAWL

With 2 strands of yarn held tog, CO 52 sts. Do
not join.
Work Rows 1–12 of Chart, or as foll:

ROW 1 (RS): k2, *yo, k1-tbl, yo, ssk, k2, MB, k2; rep from *
to last 2 sts, k2—58 sts.

ROW 2 (WS): p6, *ssp, p7; rep from * to last 7 sts, ssp,
p5—52 sts rem.

ROW 3: k2, *yo, k1-tbl, yo, k2, ssk, k3; rep from * to last
2 sts, k2—58 sts.

ROW 4: p4, *ssp, p7; rep from * to end—52 sts rem.

ROW 5: k2, *k1-tbl, yo, k4, ssk, k1, yo; rep from * to last
2 sts, k2—58 sts.

ROW 6: p3, *ssp, p7; rep from * to last st, p1—52 sts rem.

ROW 7: k2, *k2, MB, k2, k2tog, yo, k1-tbl, yo; rep from *
to last 2 sts, k2—58 sts.

ROW 8: p5, *p2tog, p7; rep from * to last 8 sts, p2tog,
p6—52 sts rem.

ROW 9: k2, *k3, k2tog, k2, yo, k1-tbl, yo; rep from * to last
2 sts, k2—58 sts.

ROW 10: *p7, p2tog; rep from * to last 4 sts, p4—52 sts rem.

ROW 11: k2, *yo, k1, k2tog, k4, yo, k1-tbl; rep from * to last
2 sts, k2—58 sts.

ROW 12: p1, *p7, p2tog; rep from * to last 3 sts, p3—
52 sts rem.

Rep rows 1 to 12 eighteen more times.

BO all sts kwise.

FINISHING

Weave in ends. Block to measurements.

NOTES

The yarn is held double throughout.

The cast-on number of stitches are on the
needle after every WS row; the number of
stitches increases to 58 on every RS row.

ABBREVIATIONS FOR SHAWL

BO bind off.

CO cast on.

Foll follows.

K knit.

K1-tbl knit 1 st through the
back loop.

K2tog knit 2 sts together.

MB (make bobble) see
instructions opposite.

P purl.

P2tog purl 2 sts together.

Rem remaining.

Rep repeat.

RS right side of work.

Ssk slip, slip, knit. Slip the
next 2 sts individually as if to
knit. Insert left needle into the
front of these 2 stitches from
the left side and knit both
stitches together.

Ssp slip, slip, purl. With yarn
in front, slip two sts individually
knitwise, then slip these two sts

back onto left needle (they will
be twisted on the needle), and
purl them together through their
back loops.

St/s stitch/es.

Tog together.

WS wrong side of work.

Yo hold yarn in front of work.

CHART KEY

☐	k on RS, p on WS
☐ o	yo
☐ ╱	k2tog on RS, p2tog on WS
☐ ╲	ssk on RS, ssp on WS

☐ ℓ	k1-tbl
☐ •	MB (see stitch guide)
▨	no stitch
☐	pattern repeat

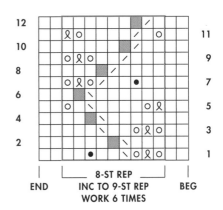

END • 8-ST REP • BEG
INC TO 9-ST REP
WORK 6 TIMES

BOBBLE STITCH

1. Knit into the next stitch on your left needle without slipping off.

2. Knit one through the back loop in that same stitch.

3. Repeat steps 1 and 2 once more in the same stitch.

4. Use the left needle to lift the third, second, and then first stitches over the fourth stitch.

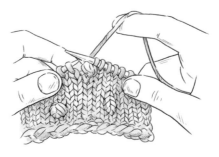

5. The bobble stitch will remain on right needle.

Fire and Ice Icelandic Cowl

Crafted with a thick Icelandic sheep's wool, this cowl will satisfy your need for a quick knit while practicing colorwork on a slightly larger scale. Inspired by Iceland, the land of fire and ice, this cowl uses traditional geometric techniques to depict the volcanic landscape as well as the snow crystals falling from the sky.

SKILL LEVEL ✕✕✕

GAUGE
- 16 sts and 13 rnds = 4in (10cm) in colorwork pattern

NEEDLES
- U.S. size 9 (5.5mm), 24in (60cm) circular needle

Adjust needle size if necessary to obtain the correct gauge.

YARN
- Bulky weight (#5 Bulky)

Shown in: Ístex Álafosslopi (100% Icelandic wool; 109yd [100m]/3½oz [100g]); #0005 Black Heather (A), #9972 Ecru (B), #0085 Oatmeal (C), and #9964 Golden (D); 1 skein each

NOTIONS
- Stitch marker
- Tapestry needle

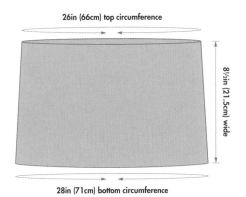

26in (66cm) top circumference

8½in (21.5cm) wide

28in (71cm) bottom circumference

COWL

With MC, CO 110 sts. Pm and join to work in the rnd, being careful not to twist sts.

Work Rnds 1–28 of Chart, working each 10-st rep 11 times across each rnd.

DEC'D RND: With MC only, *k9, k2tog; rep from * to end of rnd—100 sts rem.

BO all sts knitwise.

FINISHING
Weave in ends. Block to measurements.

CHART KEY

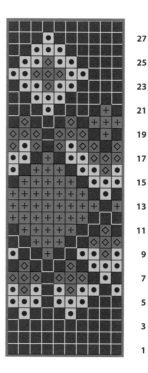

- A
- B
- C
- D
- pattern repeat

ABBREVIATIONS FOR COWL

BO bind off.
CO cast on.
Dec'd decreased.
K knit.

K2tog knit 2 sts together.
MC main color.
Pm place marker.
Rem remaining.

Rep repeat.
Rnd/s round/s.
St/s stitch/es.

Fire and Ice Icelandic Mittens

As the second piece in this matching Icelandic set (see page 62), these mittens are worked with the same thick wool, the fiber for which Iceland has become known, as the cowl. This pattern will introduce you to thumb gussets and the decreases needed to craft the perfect pointed tip on your Icelandic mitts.

SKILL LEVEL XXX

GAUGE

- 6 (7, 8)in [15 (18, 20.5)cm] hand circumference and 8½ (9½, 11¼)in [20.5 (23, 28.5)cm] long

NEEDLES

- U.S. size 7 (4.5mm) set of 4 or 5 double-pointed needles
- U.S. size 9 (5.5mm) set of 4 or 5 double-pointed needles

Adjust needle size if necessary to obtain the correct gauge.

YARN

- Bulky weight (#5 Bulky)

Shown in: Ístex Álafosslopi (100% Icelandic wool; 109 yards [100m]/3½oz [100g]); #0005 Black Heather (A), #9972 Ecru (B), #0085 Oatmeal (C), and #9964 Golden (D); 1 skein each

NOTIONS

- Stitch markers
- Waste yarn
- Tapestry needle

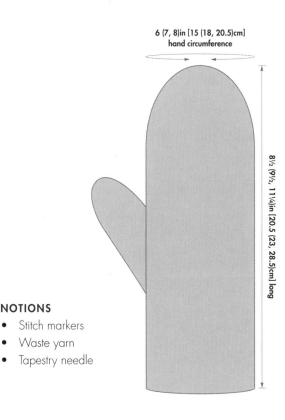

6 (7, 8)in [15 (18, 20.5)cm] hand circumference

8½ (9½, 11¼)in [20.5 (23, 28.5)cm] long

MITTENS

With smaller dpn and A, CO 24 (28, 32) sts. Pm and join to work in the rnd, being careful not to twist sts.

Rnd 1: *k1-tbl, p1-tbl; rep from * to end of rnd.

Rep last rnd until piece measures about 2in (5cm).

Change to larger dpn.

Work Rnds 1–5 of Chart A, working 4-st rep 6 (7, 8) times across each rnd.

THUMB GUSSET

SET-UP (INC'D) RND: k1, M1R, k1, M1L, pm for thumb gusset, knit to end of rnd—26 (30, 34) sts.

Knit 2 rnds.

INC'D RND: k1, M1R, knit to marker, M1L, sm, knit to end of rnd—2 sts inc'd.

Rep last 3 rnds 1 (2, 3) more time(s)—30 (36, 42) sts, with 8 (10, 12) sts between marker for thumb gusset.

NEXT RND: Place first 8 (10, 12) sts on waste yarn for thumb, CO 2 sts using Backward Loop method, then knit to end of rnd—24 (28, 32) sts rem.

HAND

Cont even in St st until piece measures 6¾ (7½, 9)in [17 (19, 23)cm] from beg, or about 1¾ (2, 2¼)in [4.5 (5, 5.5)cm] short of desired length.

Work Rows 1–4 of Chart B, working each 4-st rep 6 (7, 8) times across each rnd.

SHAPE TOP

SET-UP RND: With A only, k12 (14, 16) sts, pm, then knit to end of rnd.

DEC'D RND 1: *k1, ssk, knit to 3 sts before marker, k2tog, k1; rep from * once more—4 sts dec'd.

Rep Dec'd rnd 1 every rnd 3 (4, 5) more times— 8 sts rem.

DEC'D RND 2: *k1, ssk, k1, sm; rep from * once more— 6 sts rem.

Cut yarn, leaving a 6in (15cm) long tail, thread tail through rem sts, pulling tightly to close hole, and fasten off on WS.

ABBREVIATIONS FOR MITTENS

Beg beginning.

CO cast on.

Cont continue/s.

Dec'd decreased.

Dpn/s double-pointed needle/s.

Inc'd increased.

K knit.

K2tog knit 2 sts together.

M1L make 1 left.

M1R make 1 right.

P purl.

Pm place marker.

Rem remaining.

Rep repeat.

Rnd/s round/s.

Sm slip marker.

Ssk slip, slip, knit. Slip the next 2 sts individually as if to knit. Insert left needle into the front of these 2 stitches from the left side and knit both stitches together.

St/s stitch/es.

St st stockinette stitch.

Tbl through the back loop.

WS wrong side of work.

THUMB

Place held 8 (10, 12) thumb sts on dpn.

Join A. Knit 8 (10, 12) thumb sts, then pick up and knit 2 sts in CO sts at top of thumb hole—10 (12, 14) sts (see page 70). Distribute sts evenly over 3 dpn.

Pm and join to work in the rnd.

Work even in St st until thumb measures 1¾ (2, 2¼)in [4.5 (5, 5.5)cm], or desired length.

SHAPE TOP

SIZE 6IN/15CM ONLY

DEC'D RND: *(k2tog) twice, k1; rep from * once more— 6 sts rem.

SIZE 7IN/18CM ONLY

DEC'D RND: (k2tog) 6 times—6 sts rem.

SIZE 8IN/20.5CM ONLY

DEC'D RND: (k2tog) 7 times, remove beg-of-rnd marker, k2tog—6 sts rem.

ALL SIZES

Cut yarn, leaving a 6in (15cm) long tail, thread tail through rem sts, pulling tightly to close hole, and fasten off on WS.

FINISHING

Weave in ends. Lightly block to measurements.

CHART KEY

A

B

C

D

pattern repeat

CHART A

5

3

1

CHART B

3

1

PICKING UP THUMB STITCHES

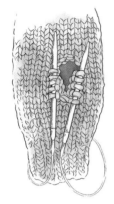

1. Place the held 8 (10, 12) stitches from the stitch holder onto the larger needles.

2. With main color, starting at the top right of the thumb gusset, knit the 8 (10, 12) stitches around the gusset until you reach the end of the row.

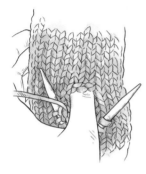

3. Once you have knit across the 8 (10, 12) stitches, you will reach the part of the pattern where you cast on two stitches. Locate these two stitches at the top of the thumb hole.

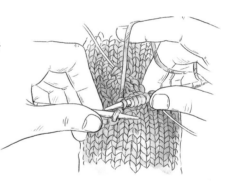

5. Knit the two stitches.

4. Pick up the two stitches. Tip: turn your work upside down, putting the two cast-on stitches at the bottom of your thumb hole. This may be helpful in picking up these two stitches.

6. You now have 10 (12, 14) stitches on your needles. Knit in the round until the thumb measures the desired length noted in the pattern.

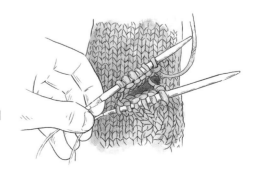

A Slow Day in Shetland Wrist Warmers

Made with wool from the Shetland Islands, this pattern was designed with colorwork lovers in mind. The simple tube design with no additional features makes for a relaxing knit, as you only need to focus on the colorwork. These earth-toned wrist warmers will make it easy to imagine picking berries in a field while the Celtic winds blow around you.

SKILL LEVEL ✕✕✕

GAUGE
- 16 sts and 13 rnds = 4in (10cm) in colorwork pattern

NEEDLES
- U.S. size 9 (5.5mm) double-pointed needles or 24in (60cm) long circular needle for Magic Loop method

Adjust needle size if necessary to obtain the correct gauge.

YARN
- Bulky weight (#5 Bulky)

Shown in: Ístex Álafosslopi (100% Icelandic wool; 109yd [100m]/3½oz [100g]); #0005 Black Heather (A), #9972 Ecru (B), #0085 Oatmeal (C), and #9964 Golden (D); 1 skein each

NOTIONS
- Stitch marker
- Tapestry needle

6 (7, 8)in [15 (18, 20.5)cm]
hand circumference

8½ (9½, 11¼)in [20.5 (23, 28.5)cm] long

— 73 —

WRIST WARMERS

With dpn or long cir needle for Magic Loop method
and A, CO 68 sts. Pm and join to work in the
rnd, being careful not to twist sts.

Work Rnds 1–90 of Chart, working chart once
across each rnd.

BO in ribbing with A only.

FINISHING
Weave in ends. Block to finished measurements.

CHART KEY

▨	A, knit
▣	A, purl
☐	B, knit
·	C, knit
●	C, purl
◇	D, knit
○	E, knit
◉	F, purl
‖	F, knit
✕	G, knit
◺	H, knit
△	I, knit
▲	I, purl

ABBREVIATIONS FOR WRIST WARMERS

BO bind off.

Cir circular.

CO cast on.

Dpn/s double-pointed
needle/s.

Pm place marker.

Rnd/s round/s.

St/s stitch/es.

An Ode to Marit Selbu Mittens

In 1857, Marit Emstad of Selbu, Norway, did something out of the ordinary. Using two different colors of fiber, she created a detailed rose design on mittens knit for her and her sisters to wear to church. This new way of knitting earned Marit the title "the mother of two-color knitting." This pattern was designed with simplicity in mind, while staying true to the traditional aspects of Selbu mittens. Intricate colorwork showcases the Selbu rose, the unique thumb gusset, and side bands.

SKILL LEVEL ✗✗✗

GAUGE
- 16 sts and 13 rnds = 4in (10cm) in colorwork pattern

NEEDLES
- U.S. size 4 (3.5mm) double-pointed needles or 32in (80cm) long circular needle for Magic Loop method

Adjust needle size if necessary to obtain the correct gauge.

YARN
- Worsted weight (#4 Medium)

Shown in: Cascade 220 Heathers (100% Peruvian Highland wool; 220yd [200m]/3½oz [100g]); #8011 Aspen Heather (MC, light gray) and #2423 Montmartre (CC, medium blue), 1 skein

NOTIONS
- Stitch markers
- Waste yarn
- Tapestry needle

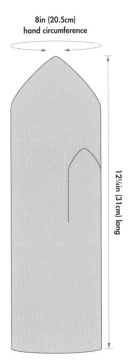

8in (20.5cm) hand circumference

12¼in (31cm) long

LEFT MITTEN

With MC, CO 48 sts. Pm and join to work in the rnd, being careful not to twist sts.

Work Rnds 1–29 of Chart A, working 12-st rep 4 times across each rnd.

THUMB GUSSET

RND 1 (set-up): Working Rnd 1 of Chart B, work first 17 sts, pm, working Rnd 1 of Chart C, k1, M1L, k1, pm, working next 27 sts of Chart B, k2tog with CC.

RNDS 2 AND 3: Working Rnd 2 of both charts, work first 17 sts of Chart B, sm, work 3 sts of Chart C, sm, then work rem 28 sts of Chart B.

Cont in established patt, work Rnds 4–15 of both charts—56 sts, with 11 sts for thumb gusset.

RND 16: Work first 17 sts of Chart B, remove marker, place next 11 sts on waste yarn for thumb gusset, CO 7 sts in colors as per Chart B, then work to end of rnd—52 sts rem.

Work Rnds 17–45 of Chart B.

SHAPE TOP

RND 46 (set-up): Work first 5 sts, ssk, work next 17 sts, k2tog, pm, work 5 sts, ssk, work next 17 sts, k2tog—48 sts rem.

RND 47 (DEC'D): Work 5 sts, ssk, work to 2 sts before marker, k2tog, sm, work 5 sts, ssk, work to last 2 sts, k2tog—4 sts dec'd.

RNDS 48–54 (DEC'D): Rep last rnd 8 more times—16 sts rem.

Row 55 (DEC'D): k5, ssk, k6, ssk, k1—14 sts rem.

Cut yarns, leaving 6in (15cm) long tails, thread tails through rem sts, pulling tightly to close hole, and fasten off on WS.

THUMB

Place held 11 thumb sts on dpn.

RND 1: Working Rnd 1 of Chart D, work 11 thumb sts, pick up and knit 2 sts in gap on left side of thumb hole (see page 70), pick up and knit 7 sts along CO at top of opening, then pick up and knit 2 sts in gap on right side of thumb hole—22 sts.

Distribute sts evenly over 4 dpn or long cir needle for Magic Loop method. Pm and join to work in the rnd.

Work Rnds 2–12 of Chart D as established.

SHAPE TOP

RND 13 (DEC'D): k1, ssk, k5, k2tog, k2, ssk, k5, k2tog, k1—18 sts rem.

RND 14 (DEC'D): k1, ssk, k3, k2tog, k2, ssk, k3, k2tog, k1—14 sts rem.

RND 15 (DEC'D): k1, ssk, k1, k2tog, k2, ssk, k1, k2tog, k1—10 sts rem.

RND 16 (DEC'D): k1, ssk, k2, ssk, k1—8 sts rem.

Cut yarns, leaving 6in (15cm) long tails, thread tails through rem sts, pulling tightly to close hole, and fasten off on WS.

ABBREVIATIONS FOR MITTENS

CC contrasting color.

Cir circular.

CO cast on.

Cont continue/s.

Dec'd decreased.

Dpn/s double-pointed needle/s.

K knit.

K2tog knit 2 sts together.

MC main color.

M1L make 1 left.

M1R make 1 right.

Patt pattern.

Pm place marker.

Rem remaining.

Rep repeat.

Rnd/s round/s.

Sm slip marker.

Ssk slip, slip, knit. Slip the next 2 sts individually as if to knit. Insert left needle into the front of these 2 stitches from the left side and knit both stitches together.

St(s) stitch(es).

WS wrong side.

RIGHT MITTEN

With MC, CO 48 sts. Pm and join to work in the rnd, being careful not to twist sts.

Work Rnds 1–29 of Chart A, working 12-st rep 4 times across each rnd.

THUMB GUSSET

RND 1 (set-up): Working Rnd 1 of Chart E, work first 33 sts, pm, working Rnd 1 of Chart C, k1, M1L, k1, pm, working next 11 sts of Chart E, k2tog with CC.

RNDS 2 and 3: Working Rnd 2 of both charts, work first 33 sts of Chart E, sm, work 3 sts of Chart C, sm, then work rem 12 sts of Chart E.

Cont in established patt, work Rnds 4–15 of both charts—56 sts, with 11 sts for thumb gusset.

RND 16: Work first 33 sts of Chart E, remove marker, place next 11 sts on waste yarn for thumb gusset, CO 7 sts in colors as per Chart E, then work to end of rnd—52 sts rem.

Work Rnds 17–45 of Chart E.

SHAPE TOP

RND 46 (set-up): Work first 5 sts, ssk, work next 17 sts, k2tog, pm, work 5 sts, ssk, work next 17 sts, k2tog—48 sts rem.

RND 47 (DEC'D): Work 5 sts, ssk, work to 2 sts before marker, k2tog, sm, work 5 sts, ssk, work to last 2 sts, k2tog—4 sts dec'd.

RNDS 48–54 (DEC'D): Rep last rnd 8 more times—16 sts rem.

ROW 55 (DEC'D): k5, ssk, k6, ssk, k1—14 sts rem.

Cut yarns, leaving 6in (15cm) long tails, thread tails through rem sts, pulling tightly to close hole, and fasten off on WS.

THUMB

Work same as for Left Mitten.

FINISHING

Weave in ends. Block pieces to finished measurements.

CHART KEY

☐	MC
☒	CC
·	purl
ML	M1L
MR	M1R
∕	k2tog
∖	ssk
☐	pattern repeat

CHART A

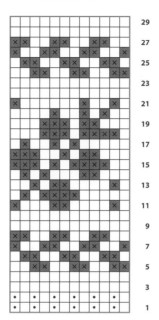

CHART C

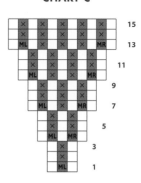

CHART D

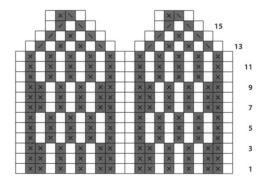

See overleaf for Charts B and E

CHART B

CHART E

Comforting Cables Fingerless Mitts

Using the cable work and seaming techniques previously covered in this book, these fingerless mitts represent a further step into detailed cabling. This is a small enough piece that you can tackle quite quickly while gaining practice as you knit.

SKILL LEVEL X X

GAUGE
- 124 sts and 37 rows = 4in (10cm) in double seed stitch

NEEDLES
- U.S. size 3 (3.25mm)
- U.S. size 5 (3.75mm)

Adjust needle sizes if necessary to obtain the correct gauge.

YARN
- DK/Light Worsted weight (#3/4 Light/Medium)

Shown in: Cascade 220 Superwash (100% superwash wool; 220yd [200m]/3½oz [100g]); #1926 Doeskin Heather, 1 skein

NOTIONS
- Cable needle
- Tapestry needle

13in (33cm) circumference

12in (30.5cm) long

LEFT MITT

With smaller needles, CO 54 sts.

ROW 1 (WS): *k1-tbl, p1-tbl; rep from * to end of row.
ROW 2 (RS): *k1-tbl, p1-tbl; rep from * to end of row.

Rep Rows 1 and 2 once more, then rep Row 1 again.

Change to larger needles.

Work Rows 1–24 of Left Mitt Chart, or as foll:
ROW 1 (RS): p1, k1, p1, k16, p1, k4, p1, k12, p1, [p1, k1] 8 times.

ROW 2 AND ALL OTHER WS ROWS: Knit the knit sts and purl the purl sts as they face you.

ROW 3: k1, p2, [2/2 RC, 2/2 LC] twice, p1, k4, p1, k4, 4/4 LC, p1, [k1, p1] 8 times.
ROW 5: p1, k1, p1, k16, p1, 2/2 LC, p1, k12, p1, [p1, k1] 8 times.

ROW 7: k1, p2, [2/2 LC, 2/2 RC] twice, p1, k4, p1, 4/4 RC, k4, p1, [k1, p1] 8 times.
ROW 9: Rep Row 1.
ROW 11: k1, p2, [2/2 RC, 2/2 LC] twice, p1, 2/2 LC, p1, k4, 4/4 LC, p1, [k1, p1] 8 times.
ROW 13: Rep Row 1.
ROW 15: Rep Row 7.
ROW 17: Rep Row 5.
ROW 19: Rep Row 3.
ROW 21: Rep Row 1.
ROW 23: k1, p2, [2/2 LC, 2/2 RC] twice, p1, 2/2 LC, p1, 4/4 RC, k4, p1, [k1, p1] 8 times.
ROW 24: Rep Row 2.

Rep Rows 1–24 once more, then rep Rows 1–8 again.

BO in patt.

STITCH GUIDE
2/2 LC (2 OVER 2 LEFT CROSS): Sl 2 sts to cn and hold in front, k2, then k2 from cn *(see page 122)*.
2/2 RC (2 OVER 2 RIGHT CROSS): Sl 2 sts to cn and hold in back, k2, then k2 from cn *(see page 121)*.
4/4 LC (4 OVER 4 LEFT CROSS): Sl 4 sts to cn and hold in front, k4, then k4 from cn *(see page 122)*.
4/4 RC (4 OVER 4 RIGHT CROSS): Sl 4 sts to cn and hold in back, k4, then k4 from cn *(see page 121)*.

ABBREVIATIONS FOR MITTS

Beg beginning.	**Foll** follows.	**Rep** repeat.	**Tbl** through the back loop.
BO bind off.	**K** knit.	**RS** right side of work.	**WS** wrong side of work.
Cn cable needle.	**P** purl.	**Sl** slip.	
CO cast on.	**Patt** pattern.	**St/s** stitch/es.	

RIGHT MITT

With smaller needles, CO 54 sts.

ROW 1 (WS): *k1-tbl, p1-tbl; rep from * to end of row.
ROW 2 (RS): *k1-tbl, p1-tbl; rep from * to end of row.

Rep rows 1 and 2 once more, then rep Row 1 again.

Change to larger needles.

Work Rows 1–24 of Right Mitt Chart, or as foll:
ROW 1 (RS): [p1, k1] 8 times, p1, k12, p1, k4, p1, k16, p2, k1.

ROW 2 AND ALL OTHER WS ROWS: Knit the knit sts and purl
   the purl sts as they face you.

ROW 3: [k1, p1] 8 times, p1, k4, 4/4 LC, p1, k4, p1, [2/2 RC,
   2/2 LC] twice, p1, k1, p1.
ROW 5: [p1, k1] 8 times, p1, k12, p1, 2/2 RC, p1, k16, p2, k1.
ROW 7: [k1, p1] 8 times, p1, 4/4 RC, k4, p1, k4, p1, [2/2 LC,
   2/2 RC] twice, p1, k1, p1.
ROW 9: Rep Row 1.
ROW 11: [k1, p1] 8 times, p1, k4, 4/4 LC, p1, 2/2 RC, p1,
   [2/2 RC, 2/2 LC] twice, p1, k1, p1.
ROW 13: Rep Row 1.
ROW 15: Rep Row 7.
ROW 17: Rep Row 5.
ROW 19: Rep Row 3.
ROW 21: Rep Row 1.
ROW 23 [k1, p1] 8 times, p1, 4/4 RC, k4, p1, 2/2 RC, p1,
   [2/2 LC, 2/2 RC] twice, p1, k1, p1.
ROW 24: Rep Row 2.

Rep Rows 1–24 once more, then rep Rows 1–8 again.

BO in patt.

FINISHING
Weave in ends. Lightly block to measurements.

Beg at bottom edge, sew together 3in (7.5cm) of side
edges using mattress st (see page 25).

Leaving a gap 2in (5cm) for your thumb, sew together
rem 1¾in (4.5cm) of side edges from top of thumb
opening to top edge.

CHART KEY

☐	k on RS, p on WS
◦	p on RS, p on WS
⧄	2/2 LPC
⧅	2/2 RC
⧄	4/4 LC
⧅	4/4 RC
☐	pattern repeat

LEFT MITT CHART

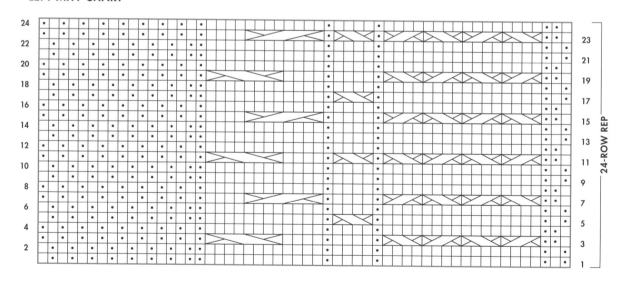

24-ROW REP

RIGHT MITT CHART

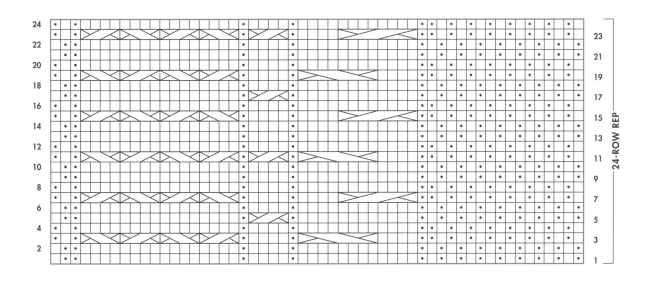

In the Company of Cables Blanket

No knitter's home would be complete without a hand-crafted blanket. Often passed down from one generation to the next, knitted blankets can act as a loving hug from someone who lives far away or is no longer around. With the amount of time and effort put into this blanket, receiving such a gift would be very special. The detailed cable work is sure to keep you on your toes and give you the unparalleled satisfaction of completing a project of this size.

SKILL LEVEL ✗✗

GAUGE
- 16 sts and 23 rows = 4in (10cm) in double seed stitch
- 23 sts and 23 rows = 4in (10cm) in center cable pattern

NEEDLES
- U.S. size 7 (4.5mm)

Adjust needle size if necessary to obtain the correct gauge.

YARN
- Bulky weight (#5 Bulky)

Shown in: Cascade Yarns Eco+ (100% Peruvian Highland wool; 478yd [437m]/8.82oz [250g]); #2445 Shire, 4 skeins

NOTIONS
- Cable needle
- Tapestry needle

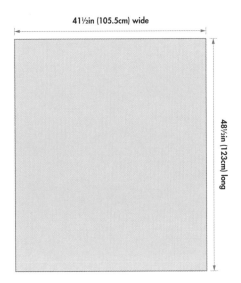

41½in (105.5cm) wide

48½in (123cm) long

BLANKET

CO 220 sts.

Work Rows 1–16 of Chart, or as foll:

ROW 1 (RS:) [k1, p1] 11 times, *p2, k3, p2, k12, p2, k3, [p4, 2/2 RC] 3 times, p2; rep from * 2 more times, p2, k3, p2, k12, p2, k3, p2, [p1, k1] 11 times.

ROW 2 AND ALL OTHER WS ROWS: Knit the knit sts and purl the purl sts.

ROW 3: [p1, k1] 11 times, *p2, T3, p2, k4, 4/4 LC, p2, T3, p3, 2/1 RPC, [22 LPC, 2/2 RPC] twice, 2/1 LPC, p1; rep from * 2 more times, p2, T3, p2, k4, 4/4 LC, p2, T3, p2, [k1, p1] 11 times.

ROW 5: [k1, p1] 11 times, *p2, k3, p2, k12, p2, k3, p2, 2/1 RPC, p3, 2/2 LC, p4, 2/2 LC, p3, 2/1 LPC; rep from * 2 more times, p2, k3, p2, k12, p2, k3, p2, [p1, k1] 11 times.

ROW 7: [p1, k1] 11 times, *p2, T3, p2, 4/4 RC, k4, p2, T3, p2, k2, p3, 2/1 RPC, 2/2 LPC, 2/2 RPC, 2/1 LPC, p3, k2; rep from * 2 more times, p2, T3, p2, 4/4 RC, k4, p2, T3, p2, [k1, p1] 11 times.

ROW 9: [k1, p1] 11 times, *p2, k3, p2, k12, p2, k3, p2, k2, p3, k2, p3, 2/2 RC, p3, k2, p3, k2; rep from * 2 more times, p2, k3, p2, k12, p2, k3, p2, [p1, k1] 11 times.

ROW 11: [k1, k1] 11 times, *p2, T3, p2, k4, 4/4 LC, p2, T3, p2, k2, p3, 2/1 LPC, 2/2 RPC, 2/2 LPC, 2/1 RPC, p3, k2; rep from * 2 more times, p2, T3, p2, k4, 4/4 LC, p2, T3, p2, [k1, p1] 11 times.

ROW 13: [k1, p1] 11 times, *p2, k3, p2, k12, p2, k3, p2, 2/1 LPC, p3, 2/2 LC, p4, 2/2 LC, p3, 2/1 RPC; rep from * 2 more times, p2, k3, p2, k12, p2, k3, p2, [p1, k1] 11 times.

ROW 15: [p1, k1] 11 times, p2, T3, p2, 4/4 RC, k4, p2, T3, p3, 2/1 LPC, [2/2 RPC, 2/2 LPC] twice, 2/1 RPC, p1; rep from * 2 more times, p2, T3, p2, 4/4 RC, k4, p2, T3, p2, [k1, p1] 11 times.

ROW 16: Rep Row 2.

Rep Rows 1–16 until piece measures 48½in (123cm) from beg, ending with Row 1 of rep.

BO in patt.

FINISHING
Weave in ends. Block to measurements.

ABBREVIATIONS FOR BLANKET

Beg beginning.	**K** knit.	**RH** right-hand.
BO bind off.	**LH** left-hand.	**RS** right side of work.
Cn cable needle.	**P** purl.	**Sl** slip.
CO cast on.	**Patt** pattern.	**St/s** stitch/es.
Foll follows.	**Rep** repeat.	**WS** wrong side of work.

CHART KEY

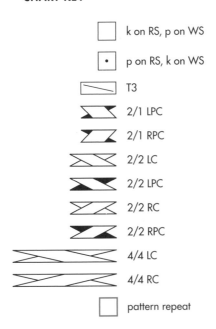

☐ k on RS, p on WS

• p on RS, k on WS

T3

2/1 LPC

2/1 RPC

2/2 LC

2/2 LPC

2/2 RC

2/2 RPC

4/4 LC

4/4 RC

☐ pattern repeat

STITCH GUIDE

T3 (TWIST 3): Sl 3 sts to RH needle knitwise, one at a time, insert LH needle into these 3 sts, from right to left and return sts to LH needle in twisted position, k3 *(see page 125)*.

2/1 LPC (2 OVER 1 LEFT PURL CROSS): Sl 2 sts to cn and hold in front, p1, then k2 from cn *(see page 120)*.

2/1 RPC (2 OVER 1 RIGHT PURL CROSS): Sl 1 st to cn and hold in back, k2, then p1 from cn *(see page 119)*.

2/2 LC (2 OVER 2 LEFT CROSS): Sl 2 sts to cn and hold in front, k2, then k2 from cn *(see page 122)*.

2/2 LPC (2 OVER 2 LEFT PURL CROSS): Sl 2 sts to cn and hold in front, p2, then k2 from cn *(see page 124)*.

2/2 RC (2 OVER 2 RIGHT CROSS): Sl 2 sts to cn and hold in back, k2, then k2 from cn *(see page 121)*.

2/2 RPC (2 OVER 2 RIGHT PURL CROSS): Sl 2 sts to cn and hold in back, k2, then p2 from cn *(see page 123)*.

4/4 LC (4 OVER 4 LEFT CROSS): Sl 4 sts to cn and hold in front, k4, then k4 from cn *(see page 122)*.

4/4 RC (4 OVER 4 RIGHT CROSS): Sl 4 sts to cn and hold in back, k4, then k4 from cn *(see page 121)*.

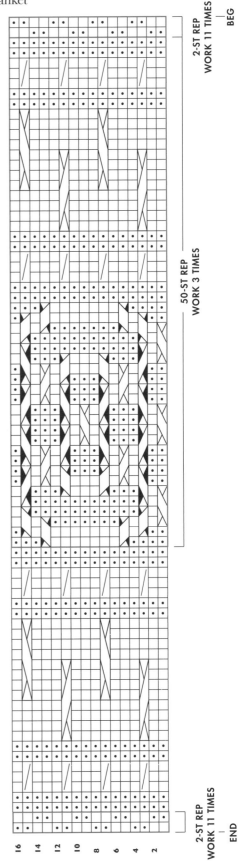

Sheltered in Scandinavia Hat

Inspired by the detailed colorwork of many Scandinavian knits, this pattern was created to expand your colorwork skills as well as pay tribute to the traditional techniques used, such as the brim folded inside the hat in order to display as much colorwork detail as possible. Use this hat as a swatch tester for the much larger matching scarf (see page 98).

SKILL LEVEL ✗✗✗

GAUGE

- 26 sts and 24 rnds = 4in (10cm) in colorwork pattern

NEEDLES

- U.S. size 15 (10mm), 24in (60cm) circular

Adjust needle size if necessary to obtain the correct gauge.

YARN

- Worsted weight (#4 Medium)

Shown in: Cascade 220 (100% Peruvian Highland wool; 220yd [200m]/3½oz [100g]); #8021 Beige (MC) and #8010 Natural (CC), 1 skein each

NOTIONS

- Stitch markers
- Tapestry needle

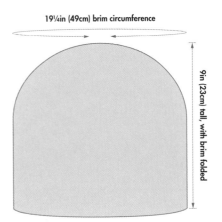

19¼in (49cm) brim circumference

9in (23cm) tall, with brim folded

HAT

With cir needle and MC, CO 124 sts.

Pm and join to work in the rnd, being careful not to twist sts.

RND 1: *k2, p2; rep from * to end of rnd.

Rep Rnd 1 until piece measures 3¼in (8cm).

INC'D RND: M1, k62, pm, M1, k to end of rnd—126 sts.

Join CC.

Work Rnds 1–40 of Chart, working 63-st rep twice across each rnd. Piece should measure about 10in (25.5cm) from beg.

Cut CC.

SHAPE TOP

SET-UP RND: *pm, k9; rep from * to end of rnd.
DEC'D RND: *ssk, k to marker, sm; rep from * to end of rnd—14 sts dec'd.

Change to dpn when there are too few sts to work on cir needle.

Rep Dec'd rnd every rnd 7 times more—14 sts rem.

Cut yarn, leaving a 6in (15cm) long tail, thread tail through rem sts, pulling tightly to close hole, and fasten off on WS.

FINISHING
Weave in ends. Block as shown (see opposite).

ABBREVIATIONS FOR HAT

Beg beginning.
CC contrasting color.
Cir circular.
CO cast on.
Dec'd decreased.
Dpn/s double-pointed

needle/s.
Inc'd increased.
K knit.
M1 make 1.
MC main color.
Pm place marker.

Rem remaining.
Rep repeat.
Rnd/s round/s.
Sm slip marker.
Ssk slip, slip, knit. Slip the next 2 sts individually as if to

knit. Insert left needle into the front of these 2 stitches from the left side and knit both stitches together.
St/s stitch/es.
WS wrong side of work.

BLOCKING

1. Lay in lukewarm water until the piece is fully soaked. Fold the ribbed section under to the wrong side of the hat so the ribbed stitches are not visible. Laying flat, line up and pin the back of the hat first.

2. Using the back section of the hat as a guide, pin the front section of hat to match.

3. This will create a double-lined brim for extra warmth. Leave the hat to dry for one to two days.

CHART KEY

- ▣ MC
- ☐ CC
- ☐ pattern repeat

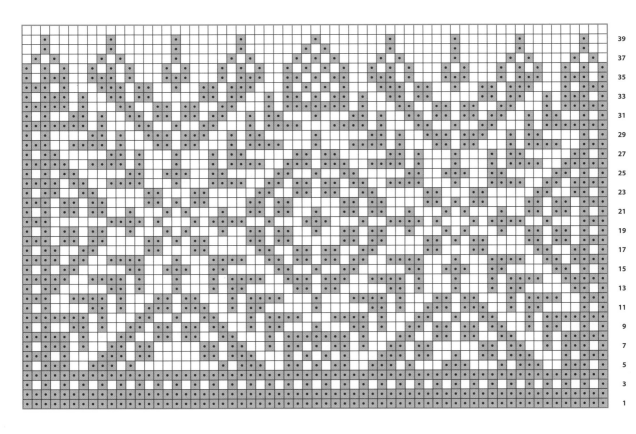

Sheltered in Scandinavia Scarf

This Scandinavian scarf requires time, but as any knitter knows, with the countless days and the care put into a piece like this, the end result is something you will certainly cherish forever. Often used in traditional Scandinavian colorwork, this pattern includes the northern flowers, leaves, and branches as well as twinkling stars you commonly find in Scandinavian knitting.

SKILL LEVEL ✕✕✕

GAUGE
- 26 sts and 26 rnds = 4in (10cm) in colorwork pattern

NEEDLES
- U.S. size 4 (3.5mm), 24in (60cm) circular

Adjust needle size if necessary to obtain the correct gauge.

YARN
- Worsted weight (#4 Medium)

Shown in: Cascade 220 (100% Peruvian Highland wool; 220yd [200m]/3½oz [100g]); #8021 Beige (MC) and #8010 Natural (CC), 2 skeins each

NOTIONS
- Stitch markers
- Tapestry needle

9¾in (25cm) wide

72½in (184cm) long

SCARF

With MC, CO 126 sts. Pm and join to work in the rnd, being careful not to twist sts.

RND 1: *k1, p1; rep from * to end of rnd.

Rep Rnd 1 four more times.

Join CC.

NEXT RND: Working Row 1 of Chart A, work 63 sts of chart, pm, then work 63 sts of chart again.

Work Rnds 2–21 of chart as established.

Working 62-st rep of each chart twice across each rnd, cont as foll:
*Chart B, C, D, E, D, C; rep from * 2 more times, work Chart B again, then work Chart F.

Piece should measure approx. 71¾n. (182cm) from beg.

Cut CC.

NEXT RND: *k1, p1; rep from * to end of rnd.

Rep last rnd 4 more times.

BO in ribbing.

FINISHING
Weave in ends. Block to measurements.

ABBREVIATIONS FOR SCARF

Beg beginning.
BO bind off.
CC contrasting color.
CO cast on.
Cont continue/s.

Foll follows.
K knit.
MC main color.
Patt pattern.
P purl.

Pm place marker.
Rep repeat.
Rnd/s round/s.
St/s stitch/es.

CHART KEY

- MC
- CC
- pattern repeat

CHART A

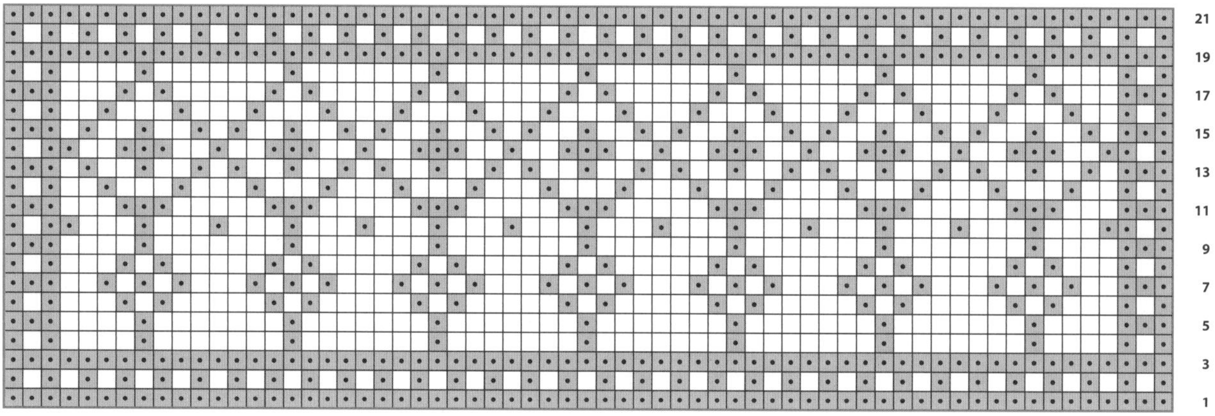

CHART B

CHART C

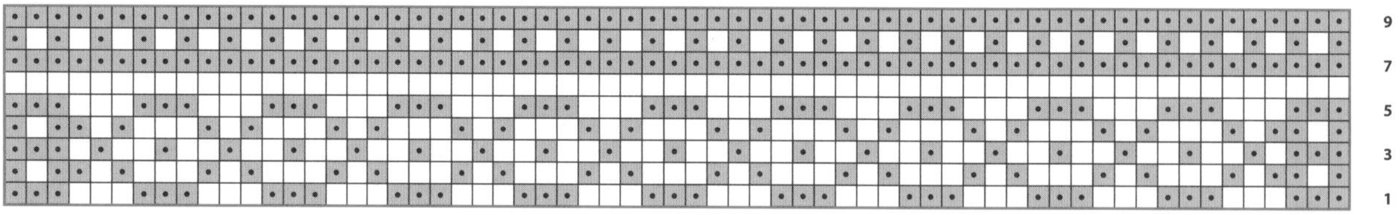

CHART D

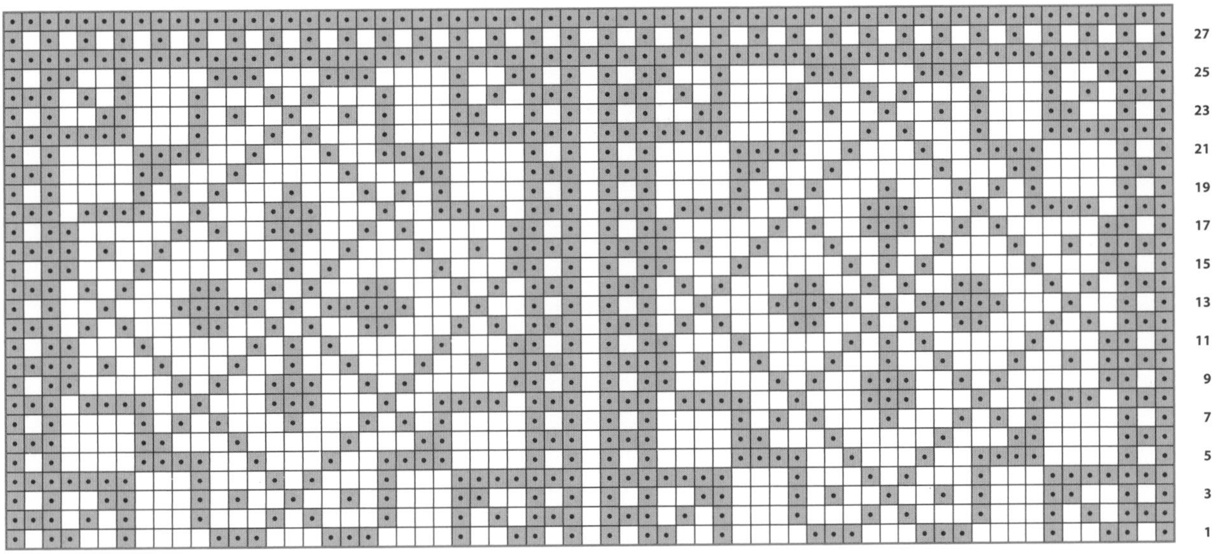

27
25
23
21
19
17
15
13
11
9
7
5
3
1

CHART E

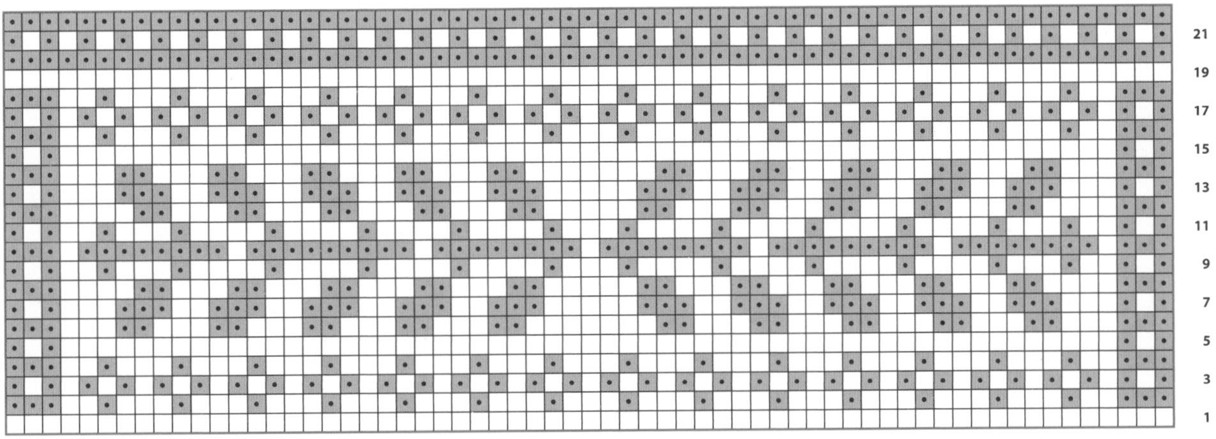

21
19
17
15
13
11
9
7
5
3
1

CHART F

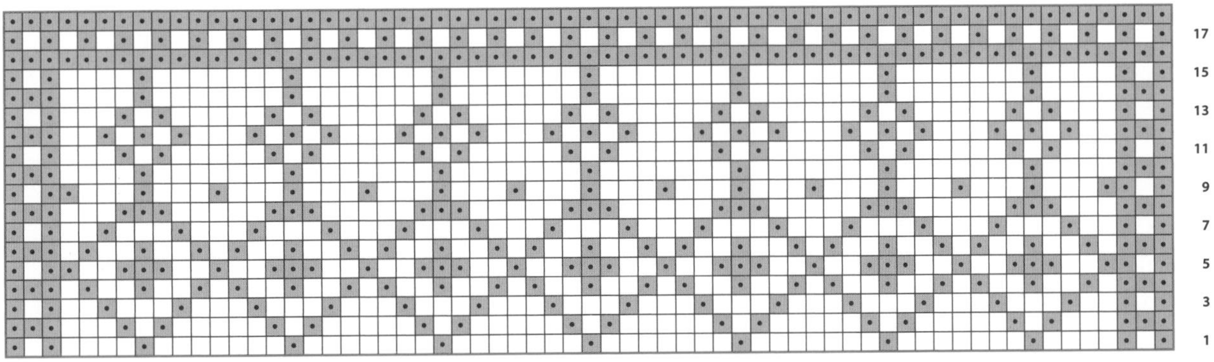

17
15
13
11
9
7
5
3
1

The Stories in Stitches Aran Sweater

Cabled Aran sweaters began on the west coast of Ireland, and have become one of the ultimate symbols of clan heritage. Many believe each clan had a specific pattern that was unique to them, which was passed down through the generations. This pattern is designed with minimal shaping and basic seaming, making it a great choice for your first Aran sweater.

SKILL LEVEL ✕✕

GAUGE

- 8 sts and 13 rows = 4in (10cm) in double seed stitch
- 44-st front cable panel = 12½in (32cm) wide; and 27-st sleeve cable panel = 9¼in (23.5cm) wide

NEEDLES

- U.S. size 13 (9mm), 24in (60cm) to 32in (80cm) long circular needle and 16in (40cm) circular needle for collar

Adjust needle size if necessary to obtain the correct gauge.

YARN

- Super Bulky weight (#6 Super Bulky) or Jumbo weight (#7 Jumbo)

Shown in: Cascade Yarns Magnum (100% Peruvian Highland wool; 123yd [112.5m]/8.82oz [250g]); #0010 Ecru, 6 (7, 7, 8, 8, 9, 9, 10) skeins

NOTIONS

- Cable needle
- Stitch markers
- Tapestry needle

See overleaf for diagrams

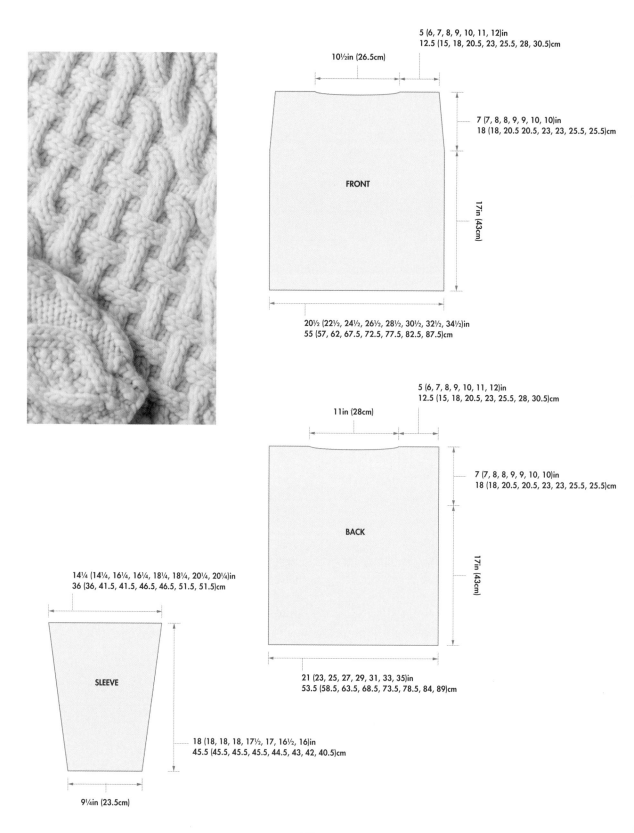

5 (6, 7, 8, 9, 10, 11, 12)in
12.5 (15, 18, 20.5, 23, 25.5, 28, 30.5)cm

10½in (26.5cm)

7 (7, 8, 8, 9, 9, 10, 10)in
18 (18, 20.5 20.5, 23, 23, 25.5, 25.5)cm

FRONT

17in (43cm)

20½ (22½, 24½, 26½, 28½, 30½, 32½, 34½)in
55 (57, 62, 67.5, 72.5, 77.5, 82.5, 87.5)cm

5 (6, 7, 8, 9, 10, 11, 12)in
12.5 (15, 18, 20.5, 23, 25.5, 28, 30.5)cm

11in (28cm)

7 (7, 8, 8, 9, 9, 10, 10)in
18 (18, 20.5, 20.5, 23, 23, 25.5, 25.5)cm

BACK

17in (43cm)

14¼ (14¼, 16¼, 16¼, 18¼, 18¼, 20¼, 20¼)in
36 (36, 41.5, 41.5, 46.5, 46.5, 51.5, 51.5)cm

SLEEVE

18 (18, 18, 18, 17½, 17, 16½, 16)in
45.5 (45.5, 45.5, 45.5, 44.5, 43, 42, 40.5)cm

21 (23, 25, 27, 29, 31, 33, 35)in
53.5 (58.5, 63.5, 68.5, 73.5, 78.5, 84, 89)cm

9¼in (23.5cm)

SWEATER

FRONT
With longer cir needle, CO 42 (46, 50, 54, 58, 62, 66, 70) sts.

ROW 1 (WS): *k1-tbl, p1-tbl; rep from * to end of row.
ROW 2 (RS): *k1-tbl, p1-tbl; rep from * to end of row.

Rep Rows 1 and 2 once more.

INC'D ROW (WS): Rep Row 1 and increase 18 sts evenly spaced across row—60 (64, 68, 72, 76, 80, 84, 88) sts.
ROW 1 (RS): [k1, p1] 4 (5, 6, 7, 8, 9, 10, 11) times, pm, p2, k6, [p4, 2/2 RC] 3 times, p4, k6, p2, pm, [p1, k1] 4 (5, 6, 7, 8, 9, 10, 11) times.
ROW 2 AND ALL OTHER WS ROWS: Knit the knit sts and purl the purl sts.
ROW 3: [p1, k1] 4 (5, 6, 7, 8, 9, 10, 11) times, sm, p2, k6, p2, [2/2 RPC, 2/2 LPC] 3 times, p2, k6, p2, sm, [k1, p1] 4 (5, 6, 7, 8, 9, 10, 11) times.
ROW 5: [k1, p1] 4 (5, 6, 7, 8, 9, 10, 11) times, sm, p2, k6, p2, k2, p4, [2/2 LC, p4] twice, k2, p2, k6, p2, sm, [p1, k1] 4 (5, 6, 7, 8, 9, 10, 11) times.
ROW 7: [p1, k1] 4 (5, 6, 7, 8, 9, 10, 11) times, sm, p2, 3/3 RC, p2, [2/2 LPC, 2/2 RPC] 3 times, p2, 3/3 LC, p2, sm, [k1, p1] 4 (5, 6, 7, 8, 9, 10, 11) times.
ROW 8: Rep Row 2.

Rep Rows 1–8 until piece measures 24 (24, 25, 25, 26, 26, 27, 27)in [61 (61, 63.5, 63.5, 66, 66, 68.5, 68.5)cm] from beg.

BO in patt.

BACK
With longer cir needle, CO 42 (46, 50, 54, 58, 62, 66, 70) sts.

ROW 1 (WS): *k1-tbl, p1-tbl; rep from * to end of row.
ROW 2 (RS): *k1-tbl, p1-tbl; rep from * to end of row.

Rep Rows 1 and 2 once more, then rep Row 1 again.

ROW 1 (WS): *p1, k1; rep from * to end of row.
ROW 2 (RS): *p1, k1; rep from * to end of row.
ROW 3: *k1, p1; rep from * to end of row.
ROW 4: *k1, p1; rep from * to end of row.

Rep last 4 rows until piece measures 24 (24, 25, 25, 26, 26, 27, 27)in [61 (61, 63.5, 63.5, 66, 66, 68.5, 68.5)cm] from beg.

BO in patt.

SLEEVES
With longer cir needle, CO 19 sts.

ROW 1 (WS): *p1-tbl, k1-tbl; rep from * to last st, p1-tbl.
ROW 2 (RS): *k1-tbl, p1-tbl; rep from * to last st, k1-tbl.

Rep Rows 1 and 2 once more.

INC'D ROW (WS): Rep Row 1 and increase 10 sts evenly spaced across row—29 sts.
ROW 1 (RS): k1, pm, p2, k4, p5, k2, p1, k2, p5, k4, p2, pm, k1.

ABBREVIATIONS FOR SWEATER

Beg beginning.
BO bind off.
Cir circular.
Cn cable needle.
CO cast on.
Cont continue/s.

Inc'd increased.
K knit.
K1f&b knit into the front and back of the same stitch to increase 1 stitch.
P purl.

Patt pattern.
Pm place marker.
Rem remaining.
Rep repeat.
Rnd/s round/s.
RS right side of work.

Sl slip.
Sm slip marker.
St/s stitch/es.
tbl through the back loop.
Tog together.
WS wrong side of work.

ROW 2 (WS): Knit the knit sts and purl the purl sts.

ROW 3 (INC'D): k1f&b, sm, p2, k4, p4, 2/1 RPC, k1, 2/1 LPC, p4, k4, p2, sm, k1f&b—31 sts.

ROW 4: p1, k1, sm, k2, p4, k4, p2, k1, p1, k1, p2, k4, p4, k2, sm, k1, p1.

ROW 5: p1, k1, sm, p2, k4, p3, 2/1 RPC, k1, p1, k1, 2/1 LPC, p3, k4, p2, sm, k1, p1.

ROW 6: k1, p1, sm, k2, p4, k3, p2, [k1, p1] twice, k1, p2, k3, p4, k2, sm, p1, k1.

ROW 7 (INC'D): k1f&b, p1, sm, p2, 2/2 RC, p2, 2/1 RPC, [k1, p1] twice, k1, 2/1 LPC, p2, 2/2 LC, p2, sm, p1, k1f&b—33 sts.

ROW 8: k1, p1, k1, sm, k2, p4, k2, p2, [k1, p1] 3 times, k1, p2, k2, p4, k2, sm, k1, p1, k1.

ROW 9: k1, p1, k1, sm, p2, k4, p2, 2/1 LPC, [p1, k1] twice, p1, 2/1 RPC, p2, k4, p2, sm, k1, p1, k1.

ROW 10: p1, k1, p1, sm, k2, p4, k3, p2, [k1, p1] twice, k1, p2, k3, p4, k2, sm, p1, k1, p1.

ROW 11 (INC'D): k1f&b, k1, p1, sm, p2, k4, p3, 2/1 LPC, p1, k1, p1, 2/1 RPC, p3, k4, p2, sm, p1, k1, k1f&b—35 sts.

ROW 12: [p1, k1] twice, sm, k2, p4, k4, p2, k1, p1, k1, p2, k4, p4, k2, sm, [k1, p1] twice.

ROW 13: [p1, k1] twice, sm, p2, k4, p4, 2/1 LPC, p1, 2/1 RPC, p4, k4, p2, sm, [k1, p1] twice.

ROW 14: [k1, p1] twice, sm, k2, p4, k5, p2, k1, p2, k5, p4, k2, sm, [p1, k1] twice.

ROW 15 (INC'D): k1f&b, p1, k1, p1, sm, p2, 2/2 RC, p5, 2/3 LRC, p5, 2/2 LC, p2, sm, p1, k1, p1, k1f&b—37 sts.

ROW 16: [k1, p1] twice, k1, sm, k2, p4, k5, p2, k1, p2, k5, p4, k2, sm, [k1, p1] twice, k1.

Cont in established patt and increase 1 st each end of every 4 rows 0 (0, 2, 2, 4, 4, 6, 6) more times, working new sts into patt—37 (37, 41, 41, 45, 45, 49, 49) sts.

Work until piece measures 18 (18, 18, 18, 17½, 17, 16½,16)in [45.5 (45.5, 45.5, 45.5, 44.5, 43, 42, 40.5)cm] from beg.

BO in patt.

STITCH GUIDE

2/1 LPC (2 OVER 1 LEFT PURL CROSS): Sl 2 sts to cn and hold in front, p1, then k2 from cn *(see page 120).*

2/1 RPC (2 OVER 1 RIGHT PURL CROSS): Sl 1 st to cn and hold in back, k2, then p1 from cn *(see page 119).*

2/2 LC (2 OVER 2 LEFT CROSS): Sl 2 sts to cn and hold in front, k2, then k2 from cn *(see page 122).*

2/2 LPC (2 OVER 2 LEFT PURL CROSS): Sl 2 sts to cn and hold in front, p2, then k2 from cn *(see page 124).*

2/2 RC (2 OVER 2 RIGHT CROSS): Sl 2 sts to cn and hold in back, k2, then k2 from cn *(see page 121).*

2/2 RPC (2 OVER 2 RIGHT PURL CROSS): Sl 2 sts to cn and hold in back, k2, then p2 from cn *(see page 123).*

3/3 LC (3 OVER 3 LEFT CROSS): Sl 3 sts to cn and hold in front, k3, then k3 from cn *(see page 122).*

3/3 RC (3 OVER 3 RIGHT CROSS): Sl 3 sts to cn and hold in back, k3, then k3 from cn *(see page 121).*

2/3 LRC (2 OVER 3 LEFT RIB CROSS): Sl 2 sts to cn and hold in front, p1, k2, then k2 from cn *(see page 110).*

FINISHING

Weave in ends. Block pieces to finished measurements.

Pm in each side of front and back, 7 (7, 8, 8, 9, 9, 10, 10)in [18 (18, 20.5, 20.5, 23, 23, 25.5, 25.5)cm] down from each shoulder for armholes. Pm along BO edges at top of front and back, 5 (6, 7, 8, 9, 10, 11, 12)in [12.5 (15, 18, 20.5, 23, 25.5, 28, 30.5)cm] from each side edge, leaving 11in (28cm) open for neck.

Sew front and back tog from bottom edge to markers.

Sew shoulders tog from armhole edge to markers.

NECKBAND

With shorter cir needle and RS facing, pick up and knit 34 sts evenly spaced across front neck, then 18 sts evenly across back neck—52 sts. Pm and join to work in the rnd.

RND 1: *k1-tbl, p1-tbl; rep from * to end of rnd.

DIAMOND CABLE

First work 2/1 RPC (see page 119) and 2/1 LPC (see page 120).

2/3 LRC

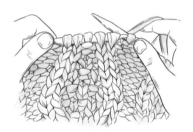

1. The starting point for this sequence.

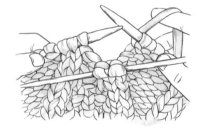

2. Slip the next two stitches to a cable needle and hold in front of the work.

3. Knit one stitch (the purl stitch) from the left needle.

4. Knit one stitch (the knit stitch) from the left needle.

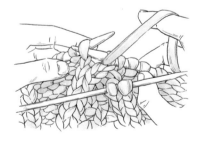

5. Purl one stitch (the next knit stitch) on the left needle.

6. Knit the two stitches from the cable needle.

Rep Rnd 1 until neckband measures about 3½in (9cm).

BO using a stretchy BO method.

Fold neckband in half to WS and sl st loosely to neck edge.

Sew sleeves into armholes, matching center of cable panel at shoulder seam. Sew sleeve underarm seams. Weave in rem ends.

CHART KEY

☐	k on RS, p on WS
•	p on RS, k on WS
	2/1 LPC
	2/1 RPC
	2/2 LC
	2/2 LPC
	2/2 RC
	2/2 RPC
	3/3 LC
	3/3 RC
	2/3 RC

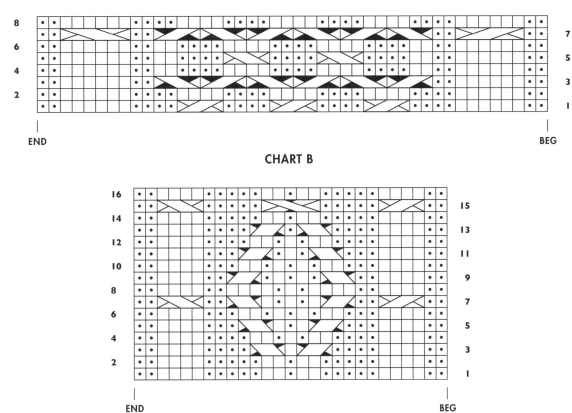

CHART A

CHART B

Hugged in Honeycomb Shawl

The honeycomb stitch is a well-known detail in Celtic knitting. Traditionally, it was an incredible compliment to receive a knitted piece that included the honeycomb stitch, since it symbolizes the hard-working honey bee, without whom the world would be lost. Adorned with honeycomb cables and twists, this piece will be extra special to give as a gift—or to keep for yourself for all the hard work you have put in!

SKILL LEVEL ✕✕

GAUGE
- 28½ sts and 26½ rows = 4in (10cm) in chart pattern

NEEDLES
- U.S. size 7 (4.5mm)

Adjust needle size if necessary to obtain the correct gauge.

YARN
- Bulky weight (#5 Bulky)

Shown in: Cascade Yarns Eco+ (100% Peruvian Highland wool; 478yd [437m]/8.82oz [250g]); #4010 Straw, 2 skeins

NOTIONS
- Cable needle
- Tapestry needle

13½in (34.5cm) wide

60in (152.5cm) long

SHAWL

CO 96 sts.

Work Rows 1–8 of Chart, or as foll:

ROW 1 (RS): k2, p2, k3, p2, k16, p2, k3, p2, k32, p2, k3, p2, k16, p2, k3, p2, k2.

ROW 2 AND ALL OTHER WS ROWS: Knit the knit sts and purl the purl sts.

ROW 3: k2, p2, T3, p2, 4/4 RC, 4/4 LC, p2, T3, p2, [2/2 RC, 2/2 LC] 4 times, p2, T3, p2, 4/4 RC, 4/4 LC, p2, T3, p2, k2.

ROW 5: k2, p2, k3, p2, k16, p2, k3, p2, k32, p2, k3, p2, k16, p2, k3, p2, k2.

ROW 7: k2, p2, T3, p2, k16, p2, T3, p2, [2/2 LC, 2/2 RC] 4 times, p2, T3, p2, k16, p2, T3, p2, k2.

ROW 8: Rep Row 2.

Rep Rows 1–8 until piece measures 60in (152.5cm) from beg, ending with Row 4 of rep.

BO in patt.

FINISHING

Weave in ends. Block to measurements.

STITCH GUIDE

T3 (TWIST 3): Sl 3 sts to RH needle knitwise, one at a time, insert LH needle into these 3 sts, from right to left and return sts to LH needle in twisted position, k3 *(see page 125)*.

2/2 LC (2 OVER 2 LEFT CROSS): Sl 2 sts to cn and hold in front, k2, then k2 from cn *(see page 122)*.

2/2 RC (2 OVER 2 RIGHT CROSS): Sl 2 sts to cn and hold in back, k2, then k2 from cn *(see page 121)*.

4/4 LC (4 OVER 4 LEFT CROSS): Sl 4 sts to cn and hold in front, k4, then k4 from cn *(see page 122)*.

4/4 RC (4 OVER 4 RIGHT CROSS): Sl 4 sts to cn and hold in back, k4, then k4 from cn *(see page 121)*.

ABBREVIATIONS FOR SHAWL

Beg beginning.
BO bind off.
Cn cable needle.
CO cast on.
Foll follows.
K knit.
LH left-hand.
P purl.

Patt pattern.
Rep repeat.
RH right-hand.
RS right side of work.
Sl slip.
St/s stitch/es.
WS wrong side of work.

CHART KEY

☐	k on RS, p on WS
⊡	p on RS, k on WS
╱	T3
╳	2/2 LC
╳	2/2 RC
╳	4/4 LC
╳	4/4 RC
☐	pattern repeat

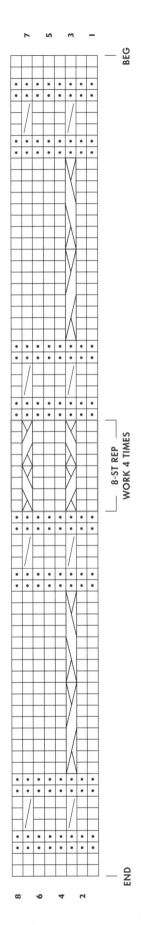

Knitting Refresher Course

The Knitting Refresher Course will help familarize you with the key knitting techniques and cables you'll be using on your journey of crafting future heirloom pieces.

JOINING IN THE ROUND

Joining in the round is a very useful technique to add to your list of knitting skills. Often used in mittens, cowls, sweaters, and hats, this technique will allow you to create a seamless tube of knitting. There are no unsightly seams on the inside of your work and there is less seaming work for you to do once your piece has been knit.

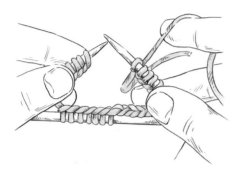

1. Bring the left (beginning of cast on) and right needle (end of cast on) toward each other, being careful not to twist the stitches.

2. Insert the right needle into the first stitch on the left needle from the front. Wrap the working yarn around the right needle and knit as you would a regular knit stitch.

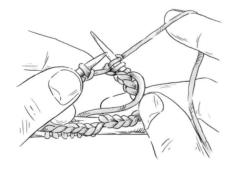

3. You have now joined your piece in the round. Continue working all stitches in the pattern.

2/1 RPC (2 OVER 1 RIGHT PURL CROSS)

The following stitch is used to cross two knit stitches over one purl stitch, in the right-hand direction, having the purl work as a background to the cable. A technique that is used in many cable designs, this stitch is bound to be useful on your knitting journey.

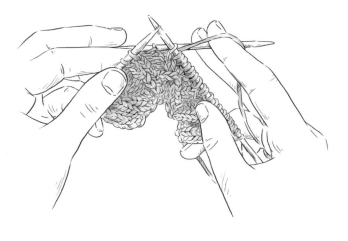

1. Slip the next stitch on your left needle onto a cable needle and hold in the back of your work.

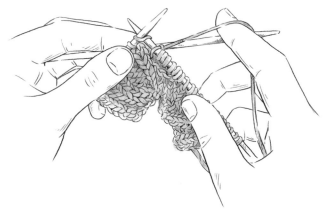

2. Knit two stitches from the left needle.

3. Purl the stitch on the cable needle.

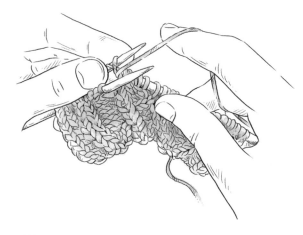

2/1 LPC (2 OVER 1 LEFT PURL CROSS)

Similar to the 2/1 RPC (2 over 1 right purl cross), this stitch is used to cross two knit stitches over one purl stitch, and moves the two knit stitches in the left-hand direction.

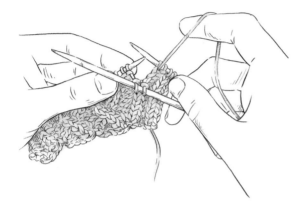

1. Slip the next two stitches on your left needle onto a cable needle and hold in front of your work.

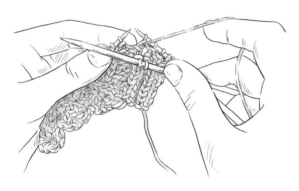

2. Purl the next stitch on the left needle.

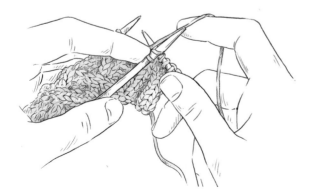

3. Knit the two stitches on the cable needle.

2/2 RC (2 OVER 2 RIGHT CROSS)

The following stitch will teach you how to cross two knit stitches behind two other knit stitches. The purl stitches in the background help to make the cable details pop. This technique will be handy to know as it is used in most cable designs.

1. Slip the next two stitches on your left needle onto a cable needle.

2. Hold the cable needle in the back of your work.

3. Knit the first two stitches on the left needle.

VARIATIONS

To work **3/3 RC**, work the instructions for **2/2 RC**, above. Instead of working stitches in sets of two, work stitches in sets of three.

To work **4/4 RC** work the instructions for **2/2 RC**, above. Instead of working stitches in sets of two, work stitches in sets of four.

4. Knit the two stitches being held on the cable needle.

2/2 LC (2 OVER 2 LEFT CROSS)

This stitch is used to cross two knit stitches over two other knit stitches to create an X-shaped cable. In this technique, the two knit stitches from the left side will be cabled under and the two knit stitches from the right will be cabled over.

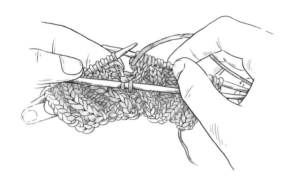

1. Slip the next two stitches from your left needle onto a cable needle and hold in front of your work.

2. Knit the next two stitches on the left needle.

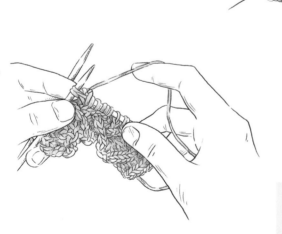

3. Knit the two stitches on the cable needle.

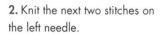

VARIATIONS

To work **3/3 LC**, work the instructions for **2/2 LC**, above. Instead of working stitches in sets of two, work stitches in sets of three.

To work **4/4 LC**, work the instructions for **2/2 LC**, above. Instead of working stitches in sets of two, work stitches in sets of four.

2/2 RPC (2 OVER 2 RIGHT PURL CROSS)

The technique shown below will teach you how to cross two knit cable stitches over purl stitches. This is used when you want to expand on where your cable is traveling on your design. A good skill to have when designing your own cables.

1. Slip the next two stitches from the left needle onto a cable needle and hold in the back of your work.

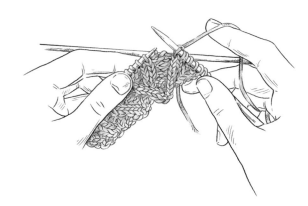

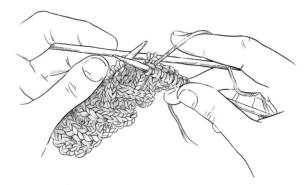

2. Knit the next two stitches on the left needle.

3. Purl the two stitches on the cable needle.

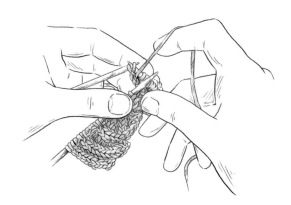

2/2 LPC (2 OVER 2 LEFT PURL CROSS)

A common stitch used in cable design, this technique is used to pass two knit stitches over two purl stitches in the left-hand direction. This technique could be used to expand the size of a cable or to create other design features you may have in mind.

1. Slip the next two stitches from the left needle onto a cable needle and hold in front of your work.

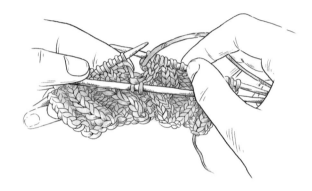

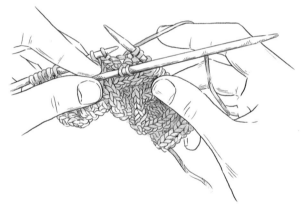

2. Purl the next two stitches on the left needle.

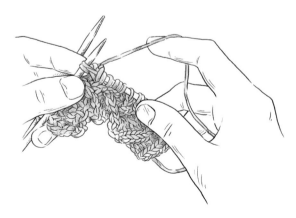

3. Knit the two stitches on the cable needle.

TWIST 3

The Twist 3 is a great technique to have up your sleeve when you want to add a little cable detail without needing to have a cable needle at hand. It's a quick and easy way to add a little extra something to your designs.

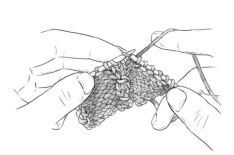

1. Slip the next three stitches knitwise to the right needle, one at a time.

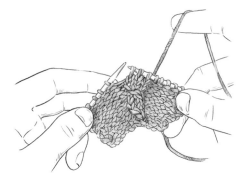

2. The three slipped stitches are now on the right needle.

3. Insert the left needle into the three slipped stitches from right to left.

4. The three stitches will now be back on your left needle, in the opposite order (twisted).

5. Knit the three stitches.

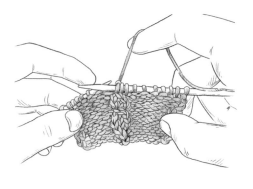

6. You have completed the twist 3.

Index

Projects are in **bold**.

Credits

With grateful thanks to Cascade for providing yarns used in the following projects:

Wrapped in Rib Scarf, *page 16*; Wrapped in Rib Hat, *page 19*; Wrapped in Rib Fingerless Mitts, *page 22*; Dream in Danish Throw Pillow, *page 28*; Mira Mhór Cowl, *page 38*; Leaves of Birch Blanket, *page 42*; Skies of Sweden Throw Pillow, *page 46*; Flowers of Finland Headband, *page 52*; White Heather Shawl, *page 58*; An Ode to Marit Selbu Mittens, *page 76*; Comforting Cables Fingerless Mitts, *page 84*; In the Company of Cables Blanket, *page 90*; Sheltered in Scandinavia Hat, *page 94*; Sheltered in Scandinavia Scarf, *page 98*; The Stories in Stitches Aran Sweater, *page 104*; Hugged in Honeycomb Shawl, *page 112*

www.cascadeyarns.com

Author credits

A special thank you to my love, Ryan, for supporting and believing in me and forever listening to me say, "Just one more row."